YOU BELONG

52 STORIES TO STRENGTHEN YOUR PURPOSE, FAITH & RELATIONSHIPS

BELONG tour

**TYNDALE®
MOMENTUM**

*An Imprint of
Tyndale House Publishers, Inc.*

Visit the BELONG Tour at belongtour.com.

Visit Tyndale online at www.tyndale.com.

Visit Tyndale Momentum online at www.tyndalemomentum.com.

Tyndale Momentum and the Tyndale Momentum logo are registered trademarks of Tyndale House Publishers, Inc. Tyndale Momentum is an imprint of Tyndale House Publishers, Inc., Carol Stream, Illinois.

You Belong: 52 Stories to Strengthen Your Purpose, Faith, and Relationships

Contents

CONTENTS

Introduction

A few months after my mother's death I had the opportunity to go on my first-ever cruise. The previous couple of years had been hard; her slow decline and eventual release had been both heartbreaking and exhausting. But now I was coming out of the fog, and a week of someone else cleaning and cooking gourmet meals for me while I sat watching the world go by seemed like the very thing to ease my aching heart.

As a cruise newbie, I was surprised by the amount of paperwork the company felt it needed before they let me embark on the ship. But I'm a rule follower by nature, so I sat down at my desk one evening to dutifully fill in all the blanks. It was the usual sort of thing: name, address, phone, etc. No big deal, right? Until I got to the question that stopped me cold: *Who should we contact in case of emergency?*

I . . . I don't know, I thought, staring at the page. *I don't belong to anybody.*

While I could make the case that I belong to God, I couldn't exactly list *him* as my emergency contact. I didn't have his phone number. Besides, if anything was to happen to me, he would already know, so there would be no need to fill him in. I briefly thought about enlisting my cat—considering that the odds of my experiencing an actual emergency were slim and it would, at least, give me a name for the form—but if something *did* happen I'd feel pretty stupid when a medical team tried to gather vital intel only to have all their questions answered with "meow." When I narrowed my choices to living humans, my options were limited: My mother was the last living member of my immediate family. I'm not married and don't have a roommate. I did have friends and extended family members who would no doubt be willing to lend their name to my form, but they didn't *have* to. They weren't ordinarily responsible for me. I didn't really *belong* to them.

Belonging is one of those things we often take for granted. Sometimes it's even annoying to be stuck with people you don't want to deal with at that moment. And sometimes (junior high springs to mind) it's the most vitally important thing ever in the history of the universe to belong to the "right" crowd (whoever they may be). But most of the time it just is. We belong . . . or we don't.

The following pages contain fifty-two stories about belonging, one for each week of the year. They address purpose, identity, and relationships (with others, yourself, and God), because all those things are seen from the perspective of where, when, and to whom you belong. Each story ends with a prayer, a thought to consider, or an idea to put into practice that week. Try not to rush from one page to the next; let the content settle into your heart and mind as you grow in your understanding of what it means to belong.

For two weeks that form sat on my desk while I tried to come to terms with my new reality. I eventually landed on a name to fill in that blank, but I haven't looked at belonging the same way since. As you make your way through the stories in this book, I hope you also will gain a new perspective on what it means to belong. Because you do. You belong with family, friends, and groups. You belong to yourself. You belong in a specific place and time, for a reason. You belong to your Creator.

You belong.

—*Susan Ellingburg, Editor*

A TIME TO TEAR; A TIME TO MEND
Nichole Nordeman

....

For everything there is a season,
a time for every activity under heaven.

ECCLESIASTES 3:1

As a newly single mom, overwhelmed by basic banking, I have been a very happy renter. Home ownership feels scary on my own, and one of my favorite people in the galaxy is my landlord, Sam, who is essentially what would happen if Santa and Pope Francis had a younger brother. I know it's time to be a big girl home owner, but I'm probably going to ask Sam and his wife to live with me and my kids.

Recently, I decided to attend the open house of a listing I'd been obsessing about. The real estate agent explained that the home was owned by an older gentleman who'd raised his family there since 1969. He'd recently lost his wife and would be moving out west to be closer to his adult children, who could help him navigate around his grief and a few less stairs.

While it had been immaculately maintained, the house had not been updated, ever. It was frozen in time. I half expected Carol Brady (or Alice, I guess) to come around the corner with a plate of warm cookies.

As good real estate agents do, they had encouraged the owner to "depersonalize" the house as much as possible. There were no family pictures. But I could see them anyway.

I could almost hear the sound of little feet in the hallway. The frustrated slamming of teenage doors. Piano lessons. The "Happy Birthday" song. And I could almost smell bread baking in the now vintage oven.

The last room I peeked in was the laundry room. There in the corner were spools and spools of colored thread, mounted on the wall above a humble little sewing table and chair, the only real evidence of the woman the homeowner had buried not long ago. Tears stung my eyes as I imagined him walking through the house with the agent, heavy and reluctant, tucking away her knickknacks and World's Greatest Grandma mugs, but ultimately refusing to put away her thread. *I'm sorry. The sewing table stays.*

I knew in an instant that she'd sewn every Halloween costume. Probably a wedding dress. She'd hemmed skirts. Replaced buttons. I knew this had been her life's work. Loving her family through the eye of a needle.

I went home making silly promises to myself that if I bought this house, I'd ask to leave the thread on the wall and learn how to use it. I'd continue her beautiful legacy. I'd update the Stone Age appliances, mind you, but I would be a seamstress. I would stitch together everything in my life that had fallen apart, like she could have. I'd make everything beautiful like she had.

When I was very small and my parents were on the tight budget of an Air Force family, my mom sewed all my clothes. She was very good at it, but I hated them. None of the other little girls had homemade clothes. I just wanted a regular JCPenney dress, like everyone else. I wore my clothing dutifully (because the only other real option was nudity), but I wasn't happy about it and made sure my mom knew.

One summer vacation, my suitcase, thought to be tied securely to the roof of our station wagon, went flying off somewhere around Albuquerque. My mom had spent months sewing culottes and matching shirts for me, and when we realized the suitcase was gone, I did such a happy touchdown dance inside. My former life as Laura Ingalls Wilder was strewn across some blessed interstate, and now there would be no choice but to hit the local mall. My dancing ended when I saw my mom's face in her hands and watched the tears come down.

It was not just the long hours at her sewing machine that were blowing across some field now, but her very heart. Every carefully chosen pattern, fabric, and stitch had been done out of love for me. I started to cry too. I wanted my dad to drive back so I could run across the highway and collect every itchy ruffled collar. I hated myself for not loving everything my mother had ever made me.

In typical fashion, my mom dried her tears and mine and dug deep to find some enthusiasm on our way to the mall. *That was then. This is now. Let's get you some cute clothes.*

In the second chapter of Mark's Gospel, Jesus is having yet another showdown with the Pharisees. They like things the old way. As part of a larger parable, Jesus offers a quick sewing lesson.

He wonders aloud, "Why would you try to patch up an old garment with a piece of new cloth? If the new cloth hasn't been treated properly (preshrunk), its fibers will be weakened. After a wash or two, it's going to tear away from the old. It's going to leave a bigger hole than the one you thought you were repairing. Don't attach me to old, comfortable things. I didn't come to fix holes.

"That was then. I'm the now.

"I'm the new."

There have been holes in my life, at times, begging for simple repair. It's harder, I think, to identify the times that beg for brand-new beginnings. When your suitcase flies off the car roof and you've got nothing left to wear. When the ghost of a woman at her sewing table (or anyone's ghost) makes you want to live her life and not your own. Trying to sew new cloth to old cloth, when you know it won't hold, because it wasn't meant to.

When the Pharisee in you says, "But, but, but . . . what about *the old things?*" the Jesus in you says, "That was then.

"Behold, I am making all things new."

PRAYER FOR THIS WEEK . . .

Lord, I can't reach out and take hold of the new life you offer if my hands are clenched around things I need to let go. I don't want my "then" to stand in the way of the "now" you have for me. Please help me determine what to hang on to and what to let fall away.

DEVELOPING CLOSE FRIENDSHIPS

Pamela Havey Lau

....

If the world seems cold to you, kindle fires to warm it.

LUCY LARCOM

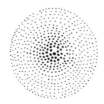

I was in my early twenties when I met a woman who modeled for me what it looks like to make friendship a priority.
I witnessed it in LeAnne Lau, my mother-in-law, a woman
who was fully alive, fully human, and yet confidently knew
her design as a friend to others. The more she nurtured me
in the art of real friendship, telling me with her life, *You have
a friend in me*, the more I realized I wasn't living the way I
wanted to and that I needed to make different choices.

As we talked over lunch one afternoon, I asked her
about her closest friends. Her eyes sparkled as she described
Heidi, Diana, Bev, and Ginger. She listed five more names
and then added another three. I knew several of these

women and said, "Mom, none of those women are anything like you."

"We have one God in common, and he's taught me how to pray for, speak the truth to, and encourage every woman in my life."

Not completely convinced of her approach, I asked her one last question: "How on earth do you find the time for all of these close friendships?"

Placing the white porcelain coffee mug on the table and looking me straight in the eye, she said, "Pam, you and I make choices every day, and prioritizing relationships is a choice to initiate, to be genuinely interested, to be transparent, and to learn to listen."

Her words helped me realize that if I wanted deeper relationships, I had to make space. I decided to back off from a hideously driven life and to slow down. I couldn't have close friendships unless I made time to listen to my friends and be present to them. . . .

If you want deeper friendships, sometimes you have to take the initiative. I discovered this fourteen years ago when I first moved to the West Coast and met Marcile. We met after she had lost her first husband to a plane crash and married her second husband, Bob. She was sixty-four years old. Marcile had a lot of family members around her, including her eighty-eight-year-old mother, three married children, eight grandchildren, and one great-grandchild. She was the matriarch and didn't indicate she needed any more friends, but we made an instant connection at gatherings, concerts, and celebrations.

I had a deep conviction to meet with Marcile more regularly. It wasn't because she and I had so much in common; our lives didn't reflect each other in any way. But there was something very present about Marcile that I knew God wanted me to witness up close and personal. I had to force myself to ask her to spend time with me at first. But finally I told her I thought she had something to offer me and I wanted to learn from her. We've met on and off for several years.

And I did learn from her. I grew, actually. It wasn't just the Bible studies we did, the books we read, or the prayers we prayed—although Marcile could exegete passages as well as any scholar I've heard. But stepping into her home, just being in her presence, calmed me. It was good for me to set aside my frantic routine of working and driving carpool and to still myself by the window in her room while she sat by me. She was always at peace, and she always wanted to tell me something about her life or herself. I discovered what women so often do in relationships like this one: I sought out the friendship for my sake but kept going for friendship's sake. I met with Marcile because I needed a mentor and ended up becoming her friend.

When Bob, her husband, died last year, Marcile had to sell their sweet cottage of a home and move into a retirement center. She called me one day and asked if I could come pray with her. As I stood in her doorway, preparing to feel her peaceful presence, I thought about our friendship: it was sweet and endearing. We could be in each other's presence without saying any words. We never ended our time together until we knew the other was encouraged.

Pursuing a friendship with Marcile took courage on my part. I initiated it. If I hadn't, our friendship wouldn't exist. And not only would I have missed out on the privilege of knowing her, but I also would have let pass an opportunity of a lifetime to be a real friend to her. My friendship with Marcile allowed me to pray for more love for her, and God gave me truths that belonged to her—truths about her person that gave so much to me.

PRAYER FOR THIS WEEK . . .

Dear God, this week would you help me to prioritize relationships? When I have a choice to make, nudge me to initiate, to be interested, to be transparent, and to listen. Friendship is such a privilege. Thank you so much for the friends I have now—and for the new friends who will come my way.

DREAMSTORMING

Kristen Welch

God's gifts put man's best dreams to shame.
ELIZABETH BARRETT BROWNING

[My husband] and I were on a coffee date at Starbucks. We knew it was going to be a good night when we scored the big comfy chairs tucked away in the corner. [We] curled up with our lattes and did something we've never done before: we dreamstormed.

"It's sort of like brainstorming," my husband said excitedly. "Except instead of writing down ideas, we're writing down our dreams. The wilder, bigger, and crazier, the better."

We didn't hold back. Some of the things on our list included working together again someday, starting a business so we could focus more on ministry, and traveling internationally as a family.

Dreamstorming is a great exercise for your brain. Normally, our brains automatically zero in on all of the impossibilities we might face if we step out in faith and obedience. With dreamstorming, the impossible is replaced with the possible. It's amazing for us to look back at that list from years ago and see a few of the things coming to pass now. Let's face it: God likes to show off.

Your sweet spot isn't some elusive mystery that God dangles over your head just beyond your grasp. It's the collision of believing in who you are and acting on it because of whom you belong to.

Little did I know that my sweet spot, a place that had become familiar, comfortable, and safe, was about to lead me to a yes I could have never imagined. But that's how God works: when we live for Him one yes at a time, He rewrites our story.

God has a unique purpose for you. Your yes won't look like anyone else's yes; it will be completely one-of-a-kind, just like you. Beth Moore explains it perfectly: "Who are you supposed to look like in your calling here on earth and in the way you follow Christ? You're supposed to look like the version of you that loves Jesus with everything in you."

That's the real you.

And that's the road on which you will find what He put you on the planet to do. You don't have to figure out what to surrender to. Just surrender your heart to Jesus. Every single ounce of it. Ask Him to give you a love for Him that surpasses anything in your human experience, a supernatural capacity. Ask Him for it every day until He does it, and then ask Him to do it some more.

If you're a writer, your exploding love for Him will bring it out. If you're a liberator, you will not be able to keep yourself from fighting to free the oppressed. If you're a teacher, you won't be able to quit studying except to share what you learned with somebody. If you love Him with your whole heart and that whole heart says sell everything and move to a third-world country, girl, get your passport!

Live Matthew 22:37: "Love the Lord your God with all your heart and with all your soul and with all your mind" (NIV).

TO DO THIS WEEK . . .

Set aside some quality time to get to know yourself and what your sweet spot may be. Here are a few questions to ask yourself to begin the process:

- *What is the world's greatest need?*
- *How would I solve it?*
- *What is the one thing I need to do?*
- *What subjects do I love reading about?*
- *What would I do for free? (List everything that you can think of.)*
- *What comes easily and naturally to me?*
- *At the end of a long day, what's the thing that I've done that brings me satisfaction?*

- *What would I regret never doing?*
- *When close friends or family think of me, what would they say my passion is? (If you don't know the answer, ask them.)*
- *What do I love about myself?*
- *What is stopping me from doing the thing I love?*
- *Am I afraid to take a risk? If so, what is holding me back? (Be honest with yourself.)*

THERE'S ALWAYS SOMETHING

Nicole Unice

....

*Every failure, obstacle, or hardship is
an opportunity in disguise.*

MARY KAY ASH

I stood in front of the book rack at the library because it's where I can breathe.

I scanned the titles and the covers, lost in the possibilities of what lies inside a good book . . . the story, the characters, the setup-conflict-resolution. A perfectly constructed sentence that unlocks a new way of seeing something that I didn't even know was important and it becomes the lesson my soul was aching to grasp.

I scan novels that promise gritty, dark plot turns and shifty characters, and then my eyes well up because I can't take any more, there's enough hard in my world to make me not want any books to open up any other ideas, any more stories that will remind me that no matter who, no matter what, I live in the grown-up world with grown-up problems. So I follow my children into the kids' section, my fingers grazing over stories that have always been a hiding place and a home base, and I long to get away from my real world because there is one thing that's true of all of us:

There's always something.

The past four weeks in the Unice home have been nutty. First I got this crazy attack that was *not* Ebola but was a pesky gallbladder situation that required surgery. Then our sweet girl got a stress fracture in her spine that requires *twelve weeks* in a full brace from her little shoulder blades down to one thigh. A variety of obstacles have jumped up at the very tail end of being done with the next book and study series that remind me in big, write-it-in-the-sky kind of ways that there is absolutely an enemy who desires to derail and destroy anything that threatens to lead people toward the love of God.

Because, well, there's always something.

Right when you think you've got things figured out, right when you think, *I am the woman who has figured out balance,* right on the day when the outfit is perfect and your hair looks good and the kids smiled on the way to school and you aren't fighting with your husband and you accomplish something at work—right on that day there will *still* be something.

I keep thinking, no matter how many times I learn, that I can avoid the *something,* that I can be strong enough or good enough or smart enough to sneak away from the grown-up problems, that I can be Encyclopedia Brown or Ramona or

Pippi or Laura in the Big Woods and that there my *something* won't exist.

I keep thinking the *something* is the obstacle, and God keeps whispering that it's my opportunity.

Choosing faith over worry.

Choosing surrender over bitterness.

Choosing to lean in rather than push away.

Choosing to live in this day rather than in the what-ifs that always, always tempt me down dark rabbit trails.

So, friend, I know you are in your something right now. You are *in it* and you don't know if you can make it through it. Maybe you, like me, are crying a little about the grown-up world with grown-up problems. Maybe you are wishing for your own Ramona story, but you are stuck with a sink full of dishes, a desk full of bills, a family full of problems, and a tomorrow full of doubt.

It's your *something*. It's my *something*.

I've been reading Hebrews 11, and this verse is haunting my every move: "Without faith it is impossible to please God, because anyone who comes to him must believe that he exists and that he rewards those who earnestly seek him" (Hebrews 11:6, NIV).

In the midst of my something, the something that threatens to steal my joy, here lies this promise. God could not have set the bar lower for faith. *He wants us to believe in him, to believe him.*

It starts with the lowest bar ever for a relationship: "Live like I'm real." He makes it the one-two punch of faith:

Believe I'm real and believe I want to love you. Believe I want to bring reconciliation to your life. Believe I want to make you whole in the midst of your something—not outside or after or around your something—right in the midst of your something.

Seek him. Earnestly seek him. Seek him with your first waking breath and your last evening sigh. Seek him in the night when you wake up with worry. Seek him when you are sitting at a stoplight, when you are folding socks, when you are eating lunch. Ask him to show himself to you. Tell him you know that he's real and he wants to show you his love in your life—today. Seek him because he promises that you will find him, that you can know him, that he has been there, will be there, and is right here in the *something*.

Go be brave. Go be just brave enough for today.

PRAYER FOR THIS WEEK . . .

Lord, help me to be brave in the midst of my something. Show me your love this week—and help me to recognize it when it appears.

ON FAITH AND WIND
Shauna Niequist

For the LORD is the one who shaped the mountains,
stirs up the winds, and reveals his thoughts to mankind.

AMOS 4:13

I grew up on the water, spending all my summers on a tiny lakeshore town in Michigan. From morning till night, we ran the beaches, soaked up the sun, picked blueberries till our fingers were stained. We shucked ears of sweet corn on the porch before dinner and caught crayfish with bubblegum and safety pins and string, and sold them for ten cents each to the bait shop.

This is what we did on regular days. But if there was wind, we sailed. We dropped everything, changed our plans. The corn could wait, dinner could wait. My mom would pack up a huge canvas tote with drinks and snacks and sweatshirts and towels, and we'd race down the marina—*Wind! There's wind!*

Both my grandfathers had sailboats in that little marina, and later my dad and brother, too. All our friends in that little town are sailors, equally happy to drop it all if it's blowing. There's a vernacular unique to sailors, a shorthand or code language that I've been hearing all my life. The phone rings: "Dad, Jim wants to know what the lake is doing."

"Tell him it's blowing 8 to 10 offshore." "Tell him it's screaming out of the north." My favorite: when it's really windy, they call it DOC—blowing so hard it could blow "dogs off chains." "It's DOC out of the NW. Get down here, dude."

The wind dictated everything, all summer long. Sailors are crazy when it comes to wind because the whole venture depends on it. If you're a powerboater, the wind means almost nothing to you. It might make things wavier than you'd like. It might make your guests spill their drinks. But for a sailor, the wind is everything, the most important thing, the center. If you want certainty, you don't sail. If you want certainty, you get a powerboat, and you stick to engines instead of wind.

I can feel that tension in myself: the tension to trust the wind or control with my own engine. I *want* to be a sailor. I *want* to trust the invisible power that's moving all the time even though I can't see it. I *want* to be patient, grounded, faith-filled. But in my fearful moments, I can feel the impulse to fire up an engine and create some motion, to pick a spot and head there fast, to burn some fuel instead of waiting around for the wind to do its powerful but invisible work.

Planning and preparation are my jam. Except for one little thing. Except for the fact that I've decided to be guided by prayer and listening, instead of planning and preparation. I've decided to learn my way into the future instead of planning my way there. I want to live by the power of the wind and not the engine.

For many years, I've had a clear path, an engine. I was often tired and a little overwhelmed by the amount of things that had to get done in a day, a week, a month. But I didn't find myself asking those fundamental questions: *What am I here for? What am I made to do?* I knew, at least temporarily, the answers. I powered along, and it kept me temporarily safe from those questions.

But now for the first time in a long time, I don't have that certainty. I'm intentionally choosing to *not know* what's next. For several years, I was too focused on working out the details of my plan to drop everything for the wind. I was a powerboater. I liked the safety and predictability of it. But I miss the rush, the freedom, the feeling of letting the wind take you wherever it will. I'm ready to drop everything for the wind again, to leave a mess, to walk away from the plan for the day—for the year, for my life, maybe, in order to feel the wind again.

This is what I know, both on the water and in my life: The wind is where it's at. When you trust the wind instead of pushing through with an engine, when you wait for life to lead and unfold in its own timing instead of shouting out your answer, when you create space for uncertainty instead of pushing for a plan, the feeling is the same: exciting and calm in the very same moment, one of the best feelings in the world.

And this is what I know: You can trust the wind. The wind takes us places we've never imagined, and it often knows us better than we know ourselves. It brings us to futures we longed for but couldn't even say out loud. I believe God is that wind in my life, that he's working all the time, and that he's good and loving.

I know how scary it can be to give ourselves over to that beautiful, terrifying wind, how hard it can be to trust the journey, but I also believe that it's worth it—that when you do, you'll feel alive and free and you'll want that feeling over and over for the rest of your life, like a drug, like falling in love.

When people ask me what's next these days, as they often do, I tell them it's all about the wind and not the engine. I tell them I'm practicing *not having* a plan. I tell them I'm trying to relearn *how to not know*, how to wait for the wind, how to trust the silence. It's awkward, and it's great. For me, these days, it's all about the wind.

PRAYER FOR THIS WEEK . . .

Lord, I want so much to be in control, but I know the journey will be so much better if I acknowledge that I'm really not the one in charge of my boat. Help me remember that I don't belong in the captain's chair; that spot is meant for you. I choose to trust that you will take me where I need to go, and along the way I'm going to practice enjoying the wind on my face.

WHEN YOU WANT TO BE THE FIXER
Amber C. Haines

....

Then Jesus said, "Come to me, all of you who are weary and carry heavy burdens, and I will give you rest."

MATTHEW 11:28

My closest girlfriends have nicknamed my therapist *Marg*, probably because I talk about her so much. I'm already an introspective woman, but it's amazing what a good therapist can cull out of you.

Once, in a good season, I threatened Marg that I'd cause trouble in my own life just to be able to keep seeing her. Sometimes I go in there and bawl my little clichéd head off, but other times I go in there and we slap our knees. We laugh hard together. I tell her my funny stories, and it feels a lot like friendship, except I pay her and she can question my motives at every turn and bold-faced call me names like *martyr*. Once I considered breaking up with her as my therapist just so we could be actual friends, but wisdom told me I'd better not.

Those are the things we think about with a smile before we go to sleep at night. *She laughed with me*, I'll think, and I hold friendships with ones who laugh and cry with me very close to my heart. I'll think about a laugh hours later, not because laughter is a rare exchange for me, but because it's an element in friendship that lightens my load. It always takes me by surprise.

One time Marg asked me about my friendships, about the role I play in them. I told her that as far back as I could remember I have been the friend to call in times of trouble. She was seeing a theme in my life. I've identified myself as a fixer, and in fact, there's not a stage I can remember when I didn't love that role. It's what I have to offer. I'm a burden bearer, the big sister, the secret keeper, and I love it.

The problem is when Burden Bearer is the only name I call myself, when I begin to think the world will fall apart if I'm not there to hold it together. Marg asked me: "Who are the friends you've called this week?" I had called the friend having a miscarriage, the friend struggling with addiction, and the friend in the middle of a divorce. I wouldn't have it any other way, and I hope these friends would call me if I were in the same situation.

Once in a while I can find myself in a particularly tough season, like the rest of you humans. My parents divorced this year, and these are things you can't always write about. I didn't want to see it in print. I didn't want it to be true, the single most painful event of my life.

It's opened my eyes even wider to how many of us are hurting in silence. Life keeps going. We're leading in churches, running meetings, folding clothes, and buying groceries with a searing wound in our hearts. In times like this it's interesting to see all the ways we hide and cope.

Somewhere along the way, I came to believe it was my sole purpose on earth to take on all the problems so those around me would be okay. If I can hold it all together, maybe I'll keep them from pain. But the truth is this: *If I can deal with their pain, then maybe I won't have to deal with mine.*

At the end of last year, I broke. In fact, this was the kindest of mercies during my parents' divorce. I was hurting and piling on the pain of others until I finally broke. I finally saw it because I literally couldn't bear up under it. I fell apart because I am not the fixer.

I am not the fixer. Say it with me.

I've prayed for help to give my burdens and the burdens of others to God, but I never really believed until this year that He is the Fixer.

To believe that God is the Healer and the light-load sharer has brought more healing to my life than I've experienced in years. It's crazy how faith in His good character will do that.

Now I call my friends simply because they're my friends. Yes, sometimes they're hurting, but equally so am I. Other times we're just laughing. My capacity to be a burden bearer is much greater now because I don't even pretend to hold up under pain. My friendships feel more whole because things don't rest on me for long. I'm a better friend because I'm taking my own heart to the Healer instead of hiding it in other people's problems. I'm a better friend because I'm closer to laughter now than I've ever been.

So tell me this. Are you a fixer? Is there a pain under all the burden bearing you're trying to ignore? I promise it's worth it to live like you're not the answer. I promise that a woman who withholds the burden from God is not the woman you should be calling in times of trouble. Call the woman who laughs. Be that woman.

PRAYER FOR THIS WEEK . . .

Lord, I'm tired of being a fixer. Deep down, I know You are so much better at that than I will ever be. Please help me hand over my burdens—and all the burdens I carry for others— to You. (And would You please help me not try to take them back from You?) Thank You.

PARIS EVERY DAY

Sarah Mae

....

We'll always have Paris.

RICK IN *CASABLANCA*

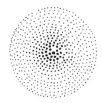

My husband is romantic, not because he brings me flowers and jewelry (I prefer books anyway), but because he sets his own life aside for me. For two years straight, he gave up all his vacation days so I could travel to write and speak. And on Saturdays he gives me the day to write or do whatever I want to do.

In marriage, romance changes, looking a bit different over time. You see a need or sense a desire and act upon it. It's practical sacrifice in the everyday things and finding ways to serve someone else. I let Jesse sleep in on Sunday mornings while I make a feast for the kids, and then he gets up. Or he brings me coffee and bacon in bed when I'm having a morning where I'm all *Everybody, stay away from me.* Or it's how we watch movies at night together. These are practical things. It's how he encourages me whenever I want to quit something, which is all the time. I get stressed out really easily, and whenever I want to quit, he'll say, "God called you to do this."

For Jesse and me, it's deeper and better and more beautiful than all the trappings of commercial ideas of love and romance. I would take our definition of romance over the romantic notion of Paris any day.

But I wouldn't turn down a trip to Paris with Jesse if it were offered. *Obviously.*

If we went to Paris together, we'd get lost.

Intentionally.

We would have zero agenda, and we would just walk around. We would talk to strangers. We'd stop and eat whenever we smelled something delicious, an aroma wafting from a café or bakery. And we would take our time. If we saw some art, we'd linger in front of a painting. If we saw a great bookstore, we'd peruse for an hour or more, enjoying no set time to be anywhere or do anything. We're not the type of people who would follow a planned, down-to-the-minute schedule to see everything. We'd eventually see all the places we wanted to see, but it would be slow and deliberate.

But the reality is, we live in Lititz, Pennsylvania, not Paris. Where do we go, what do we see, how can we capture a sense of Paris here?

I'm learning to capture it in the seemingly insignificant moments.

For example, the other night my husband came home late

from work. I was tired and the kids were sick, but I thought, *It's a moment.* I played a love song and I walked over to him and snuck into his chest. He took my hand in his, put his arm around my waist, and we danced.

The kids giggled and tried to break in, but we just steadied ourselves together.

Later that night we argued about something, and life moved past the romance, but for that moment we brought Paris into our living room. And it was tender and lovely.

Paris is in the details. Taking my husband's hand when I could easily just be content without touching him. Choosing to kiss him a little longer than usual. Playing footsie with him at the movie theater or at dinner. Savoring the food when we're out, and laughing just a little too loud at his jokes. Letting him know that even though life and marriage can be frustrating as anything, it is still ours, and that matters.

Paris is taking the time to let imperfect love still matter.

And when we finally do go to Paris one day, we will enjoy every walk, every dance, every hand-hold, every kiss, every footsie, and every bite of delectable food, just as we do at home.

Yeah, it's ugly sometimes in my house, and I'm selfish, and stretching into love with a sinner you have to sleep next to is such a crazy, ridiculous thing. But that crazy thing is God's idea, and so it matters.

So we celebrate.

We dance.

And once in a while, we even let the kids break in.

TO DO THIS WEEK . . .

How can you bring "Paris" into your everyday life? Whether it's a moment you share with your husband, families, or friends, look for moments to let the people you love know that they matter.

WHEN LIFE FEELS LIKE A MESS, THERE'S SOMETHING WE CAN DO

Rachel Macy Stafford

....

I now see how owning our story and loving ourselves through
that process is the bravest thing that we will ever do.
BRENÉ BROWN

My friend lost her sister to cancer four months ago. She talks about it—the pain and disbelief, the pressure to move on, the things that help and the things that don't. She talks about the good days and the indescribably bad days.

I listen to everything she offers. I tuck it away for safekeeping. With her help, I'll know a better thing to say when someone hurts. With her help, I have some perspective on inconsequential problems when they're getting more attention than they deserve.

Each time my friend shares, I am struck by admiration and awe. I think to myself, *She never wanted to be the messenger; she never wanted to be an expert on grief; she never wanted to know what words, what actions bring a moment of solace to an aching soul.*

But she is. And she does.

This is now my friend's story, and as much as she'd like to deny it, she's chosen to own it—quite bravely and brilliantly, I might add.

I thought of my friend and her unchosen expertise when I had a CT scan in June. It was the first time I lay beneath a big scary machine and held my breath for dear life. When the machine began to inch forward slowly, I thought of my friend and her story. I wasn't sure how my story was going to play out, but I decided I would own it. Tell my close friends what I was going through. Say, "I'm scared," when I felt scared. Ask for help when I was in pain. Above all, I knew it was important to pay attention. So I vowed to take it all in—the good and bad—and perhaps discover something worth sharing in the process.

Four weeks after the CT scan that saved my left kidney and possibly my life, I was home from the hospital. I was swollen and sore. I was groggy on pain meds. I was having trouble thinking of words. I was kind of a mess. But I had something I felt must be said. I pulled my laptop computer gingerly onto my lap and typed some words to my friends and family on social media. I remember worrying for a brief moment that there might be incomplete sentences, misspelled words, and extra periods. Words were blurry through my grateful, teary eyes, but I pushed "publish" anyway. Here is an excerpt:

I am home from the hospital recovering from kidney surgery and feeling incredibly thankful to be here. It's been many months of infection and uncertainty, but I finally have peace. I am on my way to more years, more love, more life. My little public service announcement in the midst of this overwhelming gratitude is this: If you feel like something is not right in your body or mind, please don't dismiss that feeling. Make an appointment today. If you are not satisfied with the answers you get or things do not improve, keep searching. Keep asking. Keep listening. Keep going until you get answers. You are the only one who can truly look after YOU. And your people need you to be HERE.

An interesting thing happened. Two of my neighbors contacted me over the next few weeks to tell me those words prompted them to action. One of them made an appointment regarding a persistent pain she'd neglected to look into. Another friend said she'd been worried about her spouse's health and my words were the perfect words to offer him.

I cried.

Though I felt like a mess, I provided a vital message.

In that moment, I felt better than I had in months. The uncertainty and pain I'd endured weren't all for naught. For the first time, I saw my story not as a curse but as a blessing. It was a blessing to be the messenger.

PRAYER FOR THIS WEEK . . .

God, help me to own my story. Give me the words and the opportunity to deliver the message I have to share, even—especially—when I feel like a mess.

GET RID OF THINGS
Regina Brett

....

Don't store up treasures here on earth,
where moths eat them and rust destroys them,
and where thieves break in and steal.

MATTHEW 6:19

Getting rid of things goes against my genetics.

My Depression-era parents kept everything. Having spent their childhood poor, they taught us never to throw anything out. Dad's garage was a temple to thrift, Mom's basement a shrine to saving. Socks with holes? Use them for rags. Shirts with stains? Wear them under sweaters. Jeans with worn knees? Cut them into shorts.

Open my closet door and you can see the family resemblance. What stops me from cleaning it is that I bump into all the me's I left behind.

The Athletic Me can't part with the kneepads, volleyball shoes, Rollerblades, ice skates, and assorted sports bras that convince me I'm still young enough to be the athlete I never was.

The Hip Me owns a black spandex skirt that looks great until I've worn it for three hours. It stretches to hug the derriere but doesn't tighten, so when you stand up it looks like you're hiding twin first graders under your skirt.

The Younger Me used to look perky as a cheerleader in the gray miniskirt with the pleats in the front. Time to let go of that and the $80 shoes with the four-inch heels that feel like I'm wearing stilts on ice.

The Sexy Me believes that one day I will look exactly like the woman on the Black Velvet billboard if I wear the black velvet padded bra or the black stretchy slip that won't let you exhale.

The Nostalgic Me hangs on to every item with a story, like the Bride and Groom baseball caps we got as a wedding gift. Can we keep wearing them? We still feel like newlyweds. Or the hot pink tunic I wore when I met the man I married. He claims it was love at first sight. Thank goodness love is blind.

The Realistic Me takes over and decides it's time to part with anything I haven't worn in five years. I pile everything to give away. A mountain range forms. I feel like a new woman. My life is organized. Well, at least my closet.

A few years later I tackled the whole house after clutter coagulated and clogged the arteries of our home. Saint Benedict once wrote that the extra clothes you store in your basement, attic, and closets belong to the poor. I'm not so sure the poor want dozens of pink fund-raising T-shirts from all those walks for the cure, but they've got them now.

For three months, I was a woman possessed, decluttering the house from top to bottom. It all started with tossing out two nasty chairs. A mustard yellow office chair and an Early American Ugly dining chair. When I put them on the curb one day I found out the neighbors were having a house sale.

Figuring I had a built-in audience, I unloaded our basement onto the curb. I tossed an old coffee table, skylight, rocking chair, stereo, and the green antique marble lamp I picked up off someone else's curb. All it needed was a cord and plug to work, but after a year sitting in the basement, it wasn't any closer to working, so out it went.

My neighbor grabbed it. Fifteen minutes later, it was back on the curb. His wife refused to let it in the house. It turns out one man's trash isn't always another man's treasure. Sometimes it's still trash.

I threw out mismatched gloves and socks, moth-eaten hats and scarves, candles that melted in storage, and fabric for a dress I pinned to a pattern 20 years ago. I didn't even stop to save the pins.

As I sorted it all, I asked myself four questions: Is it useful? Is it beautiful? Does it add meaning to your life now? If this item were free at a garage sale, would you take it? That last question served as a truth serum. Most everything got tossed.

I filled the curb and strangers emptied it. By noon, it was all gone. The house felt ready now. For what, I would find out as time went on.

Decluttering forces you to let go of the past. It creates an opening for the future. What are you making room for? New ways to experience leisure and romance, creativity and serenity. New hobbies, new friends, new goals. Once you evict the excess, you can embrace the essentials: that which is beautiful, meaningful, and enhances your life.

When you finally let go of the person you used to be, you get to discover the person you are now and the person you want to become.

TO DO THIS WEEK . . .

Look at things in your home—you might want to start with one closet—and ask yourself the following questions about each item: Is it useful? Is it beautiful? Does it add meaning to your life now? If this item were free at a garage sale, would you take it? If the answer to any of these questions is "no" . . . get rid of it.

I'M STILL LEARNING TO FORGIVE

Corrie ten Boom

···

If you forgive those who sin against you, your heavenly
Father will forgive you. But if you refuse to forgive others,
your Father will not forgive your sins.

MATTHEW 6:14-15

It was in a church in Munich that I saw him, a balding heavyset man in a gray overcoat, a brown felt hat clutched between
his hands. People were filing out of the basement room where
I had just spoken, moving along the rows of wooden chairs to
the door at the rear. It was 1947 and I had come from Holland
to defeated Germany with the message that God forgives.

It was the truth they needed most to hear in that bitter,
bombed-out land, and I gave them my favorite mental picture. Maybe because the sea is never far from a Hollander's
mind, I liked to think that's where forgiven sins were thrown.
"When we confess our sins," I said, "God casts them into the
deepest ocean, gone forever."

The solemn faces stared back at me, not quite daring to believe. There were never questions after a talk in Germany in 1947. People stood up in silence, in silence collected their wraps, in silence left the room.

And that's when I saw him, working his way forward against the others. One moment I saw the overcoat and the brown hat; the next, a blue uniform and a visored cap with its skull and crossbones. It came back with a rush: the huge room with its harsh overhead lights, the pathetic pile of dresses and shoes in the center of the floor, the shame of walking naked past this man. I could see my sister's frail form ahead of me, ribs sharp beneath the parchment skin. Betsie, how thin you were!

Betsie and I had been arrested for concealing Jews in our home during the Nazi occupation of Holland; this man had been a guard at Ravensbrück concentration camp where we were sent.

Now he was in front of me, hand thrust out: "A fine message, *Fräulein*! How good it is to know that, as you say, all our sins are at the bottom of the sea!"

And I, who had spoken so glibly of forgiveness, fumbled in my pocketbook rather than take that hand. He would not remember me, of course—how could he remember one prisoner among those thousands of women?

But I remembered him and the leather crop swinging from his belt. It was the first time since my release that I had been face to face with one of my captors, and my blood seemed to freeze.

"You mentioned Ravensbrück in your talk," he was saying. "I was a guard there." No, he did not remember me.

"But since that time," he went on, "I have become a Christian. I know that God has forgiven me for the cruel things I did there, but I would like to hear it from your lips as well. *Fräulein*—" again the hand came out—"will you forgive me?"

And I stood there—I whose sins had every day to be forgiven—and could not. Betsie had died in that place— could he erase her slow terrible death simply for the asking?

It could not have been many seconds that he stood there, hand held out, but to me it seemed hours as I wrestled with the most difficult thing I ever had to do.

For I had to do it—I knew that. The message that God forgives has a prior condition: that we forgive those who have injured us. "If you do not forgive men their trespasses," Jesus says, "neither will your Father in heaven forgive your trespasses."

I knew it not only as a commandment of God, but as a daily experience. Since the end of the war I had had a home in Holland for victims of Nazi brutality. Those who were able to forgive their former enemies were able also to return to the outside world and rebuild their lives, no matter what the physical scars. Those who nursed bitterness remained invalids. It was as simple and as horrible as that.

And still I stood there with the coldness clutching my heart. But forgiveness is not an emotion—I knew that too. Forgiveness is an act of the will, and the will can function regardless of the temperature of the heart. *"Jesus, help me!"* I prayed silently. *"I can lift my hand. I can do that much. You supply the feeling."*

And so woodenly, mechanically, I thrust my hand into the one stretched out to me. And as I did, an incredible thing took place. The current started in my shoulder, raced down my arm, sprang into our joined hands. And then this healing warmth seemed to flood my whole being, bringing tears to my eyes.

"I forgive you, brother!" I cried. "With all my heart!"

For a long moment we grasped each other's hands, the former guard and the former prisoner. I had never known God's love so intensely as I did then.

THOUGHT FOR THIS WEEK . . .

Think about what it means to be forgiven. If you were in Corrie's place, would you be able to forgive the former guard? If you were in his place, would you ask for forgiveness? Would you accept forgiveness if it was offered?

THE WEB

Patsy Clairmont

....

Habits are cobwebs at first; cables at last.

CHINESE PROVERB

Intertwined with the precision of an ancient weaver, the threads hanging outside my office window were beaded with morning dew. The silky filaments draped between two narrow pines. The web waited in daylight for unsuspecting "flyers," while the spider poised in the dark caves of tree limbs, ready to pounce.

At dusk the spider emerged to repair tears made by victims and weather. I watched as its body produced a thin strand that it dangled from like a trapeze artist. It deftly used its legs to securely devise—in thin air—the almost invisible snare.

I pondered this wonder through glass, amazed at the

treachery of it. It reminded me that our enemy Satan sets traps, hoping for pouncing opportunities.

Early in my life the enemy crocheted webbed indictments against my personal value into my thoughts, and then in vulnerable moments he dangled them to see if I'd get caught up in the stickiness of self-defeat or the silken-sickness of self-pity. And I did.

Wound up in a cocoon of fear and shame, I believed I didn't deserve to feel good about who I was—or that I could possibly be loved by God. And not only did I buy into the lies, I helped keep them circulating inside my identity through repetition. I thought if God loved me, my life would be better, easier, healthier—and it wasn't.

Until . . .

I was willing to do the hard work of recovery. I began to risk the thought that not only might God love me, maybe he had a way out of the dark cave I later would learn I helped to create. God was my last-ditch effort for sanity and dignity. But I would need to deliberately take steps toward light; the light of God's Word, the light of honesty, the light of change. Thankfully, he makes a way of escape for us laced with morning mercies and daily grace.

Satan's lies were woven so firmly into my beliefs that it took the Holy Spirit illuminating the counsel in Scripture to help me break vicious cycles of accusations aimed at my demise. I began memorizing verses that would in time help me to replace the seething indictments with God's tender regard for me. The more Scripture I processed, the more sure was my faith. A certainty began to grow within me that I could trust God even when I felt alone, misunderstood, fearful, and melancholy.

I also had to deliberately move my muscles. I found sitting in my fear and sadness kept me victimized by the tyranny of self-hatred, while accomplishments (making my bed, getting dressed, washing dishes) helped restore personal worth.

I gradually began to self-nurture as I made wise and uplifting choices: by the friendships I developed, the music I listened to, the books I read, and the habits I upgraded (reducing coffee intake, giving up cigarettes, moderating TV time, and filling my idle hours with worthy efforts like gardening, photography, writing, painting, etc.).

As I ventured out of my seclusion, I shook loose more of the enemy's web by joining a Bible study, a self-help group, a prayer group, and a church family. I learned that we were meant to be connected to others. People modeled for me friendship, discipleship—even sanity.

My identity recovery has taken a lifetime. I've now entered my seventies, and I am aware I still have to be careful of the allure of sticky-silver threads in the wind.

PRAYER FOR THIS WEEK . . .

God, sometimes the webs we're caught in are so hard to see. Show me where I have become entangled in things that are not good for me. Help me make better choices so that I can be free to be all that you made me to be.

THE AGE OF FRIENDS
Sarah Zacharias Davis

....

*A friend is one to whom one may pour out the contents of one's
heart, chaff and grain together, knowing that gentle hands
will take and sift it, keep what is worth keeping, and with a
breath of kindness blow the rest away.*

GEORGE ELIOT

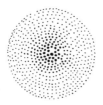

From time to time I look back over pieces from my previous
friendships: birthday cards, letters, and poems, and photo-
graphs of Christmas gift exchanges, homecomings, gradua-
tions, and late nights of sleep-deprived hilarity. I look back
over those memories with nostalgia. I see myself in those pictures and think how young I was then. Not so much young
in years, though I was that, too, but young in life experience
and wisdom.

Sometimes I think it's sad that later we get so caught up
in the business of living life that we often don't really live
life. We spend our time *doing* so that we can eventually start
living. But it's not only mere busyness, of course; adult life

makes legitimate demands of us. The truth of the matter is that priorities often change; they need to change for the sake of the relationships and responsibilities we have chosen for ourselves. We make new friends at our places of work or our children's school, or with the wives of our husband's friends, and that is certainly not a bad thing.

But we hold the age of friendship with sacredness, if we ever stop to think of it, in part because, though those friendships were the center of our world, we didn't really appreciate them until the age had passed. Even when we are consumed with demands that take priority over friendships, we hold a greater appreciation for those relationships, both past and current. Those friends knew so much more of our lives because we spent so much time together. They saw far more of our ups and downs, our messiness. Often those friends knew us before we learned to conceal our messiness so well. That was when we dreamed about the life we would have, before we actually thought we had it or realized we weren't going to. That was when we thought we could do anything, be anything, accomplish anything, and have everything.

Our friends sat with us when we divulged the exhaustive details of the first date with the man who was later to be our husband, when we realized we hated the major we were two years into, and when we broke off our first serious relationship. They were with us when we had impossibly unreal expectations for our bodies, figured out what we were going to be when we grew up, got our first "real job," bought clothes that weren't on sale, and stepped over the threshold from coed to woman.

But I'm starting to think the age of friendship comes back around. "Every real Friendship is a sort of secession, even a rebellion," says C. S. Lewis. Perhaps later in life we have the courage again to stage that rebellion. We seem to have a renewed appreciation for the age of friendship when it returns the way fashion trends from decades ago do—like capri pants, skinny jeans, and miniskirts. Our friends no longer define us as they once did, but we now choose friends for how we are drawn to them, and they are very much a part of us.

And while the rule of fashion is that one should not attempt to wear a trend when it makes its return the second, or perhaps third, time around, we are never too old for friendships. In the second age of friendship, our friends sit beside us as we struggle to keep a marriage fresh and alive and champion us when we finally get the promotion to senior management or purchase the home we'll probably live in for the next few decades of our lives. They engage with us as we rethink so much of what we thought was true about life when we were younger. And later they come alongside us as we care for aging parents, as our children leave us, when we learn we have breast cancer, and as we maneuver grandparenting and adjust to being around young children again. These are the friends we live life alongside with a sense of humor, having finally learned that we just can't take ourselves too seriously anymore, the way we once did.

In the tender first age of friendships, those girls were our lives, but in the second age, they are women who help us navigate what has actually become our lives.

TO DO THIS WEEK . . .

Think about the friends in your life. Have you told them lately what they mean to you? This week would be a good time to do that. Send a card, text, or e-mail; pick up the phone and call, Skype, or FaceTime; the method doesn't matter as much as the message that you care.

RENEWED DAY BY DAY

Rebecca S. Sandberg

....

When you pray, move your feet.
AFRICAN PROVERB

Somewhere in the places of my yesterdays, I found myself at age twenty-five living in Nairobi. Had I known this would have been the case, I might have taken strides to—well—be someone else. My husband and I arrived in Kenya with our baby boy and six duffle bags. It was July. Nairobi is below the equator, so Kenyan "winter" was upon us—with cool rain and pleasant days.

One of my first observations when meeting relief workers and field "staffers" was that most relief workers who were men were married to relief working nurses or doctors—people who truly bring lifesaving skills to humanity. The observation sat dormant in my mind for a week or two, and then I began to panic. My husband is a relief worker. Who am I?

I can say with some confidence that my brain is not wired for medicine or science. I pondered long and hard about my lack of medical savvy and made a declaration to pursue something of a medical-nursing-doctor-ish nature. The Lord, in his infinite wisdom and love, spared patients the world over from my declaration and led me down another path—a literal path, dusty and straight, papaya trees on one side and avocado trees on the other. The rhythm of women singing a Swahili song kept my feet walking. Their chorus swelled and ended in unison, "Hallelujah, Amen!" There I was, surrounded by about fifty women, who I learned were refugees.

They were part of a micro-enterprise that taught sewing. They had a thriving shop and a flourishing community. I spent the better part of five years working at this place. I found that all of the space in my brain that clearly was not wired for medicine was actually wired for creativity and art.

After many years, I said my tear-laden good-byes and left on the same dusty path that had brought me there. My husband, our two sons, and pregnant-me headed to a place definitely above the equator—Illinois. Within a few short months of arriving, "winter" was upon us, literally and emotionally.

I found myself thinking of Kenya and trying to take myself back, if only in my imagination. One January night, I drove to Target to get some diapers. It was snowing, of course. I was in a foul mood and wrestled out loud with God as to why he brought us to this place. I made my way through a sea of pasty people who were also at Target to pick up the "necessities" of life. Then I returned to my car and said in a rather sarcastic way, "Oh, good Lord. Help."

In my experience, taking this type of attitude to God never bodes well.

Still huffing, I left the parking lot. Through my snowy windshield, I saw someone walking on the side of the road. As I got closer, I saw that she was wrapped in African Kitenge cloth and was wearing flip-flops. She turned into an apartment complex and, yes, I followed her; what's more, I knocked on her door.

I was greeted with the smell of familiar spices, the sound of lots of children, and a smiling woman, called Mwambe. Had I not been aware of the chill behind me, I might have thought I was in Nairobi again. Mwambe invited me in and we talked and laughed. After a while, I decided to go, and I gave her a hug.

"You can give me job?" she said.

I fumbled through a sentence of strange words that really meant nothing and left, closing the door behind me.

Pause. No, seriously, I paused for a long time, snow accumulating on my head. That night God spun my affections like a top on a table, round and round and round. For months, I thought of Mwambe. I learned the facts, the numbers, and the needs of refugees who come to America. One of the greatest needs for refugees is employment. My husband and I began to talk, pray, and ponder.

In 2009, The Re:new Project was birthed out of a desire to empower refugee women to gain a viable skill and employment within a safe community of women. What started in a small room with five machines and a few students is now a thriving community of employees who create beautiful products. Working alongside refugees over the last ten years has profoundly changed my life. They are my teachers. They are brave, courageous, and strong. The story behind The Re:new Project is a story about how living in community is the only way to live. It is about how God helps us while we are here on this earth—creating, living, and loving—being renewed day by day.

PRAYER FOR THIS WEEK . . .

Oh, Good Lord: Help. Help me see that my gifts may not be the same as those of the people around me . . . and that's okay. After all, you didn't create me to be them; you made me to be me. Show me how I can use the skills you have given me to help others in a way that pleases you.

FOUR STAGES OF ROAD TRIP MANAGEMENT

Jen Hatmaker

Those that say you can't take it with you never saw a car
packed for a vacation trip.

UNKNOWN

I have five kids. It's just a big number, and they all live with us. *All* of them. But my oldest son is a senior this year and I'm starting to just freak out a little bit like, *Oh my word, it went too fast.* I hated it when moms told me that when my kids were little, and it happened! So I said to my husband, Brandon, "Baby, we are running out of time. I mean *this is it* with this kid. We've got to cram in some family memories. Okay? The runway has shortened up here. What we need to do is—we need some road trips this summer."

And so this summer we loaded our kids up in the car, and we decided to take an eleven-hour road trip to Missouri.

Have you traveled with your people? Did you ever think at that moment, *Whose idea was this?*

Brandon told me the night before, "Hey, in the morning, we're leaving at 8 a.m. sharp." I said, "Baby, we're half-packed. We've got to get a dog to the kennel. We have a thousand moving parts. There is a zero percent chance we are leaving at 8 a.m."

And he was like, "You know what, we're leaving at 8 a.m., and I'll tell you why: We're the parents, and these children have to do what we say. We are not ruled by this army that we have created." So the next morning we pulled out just shy of ten. Brandon was speaking to none of us. There was no communication going in the car. It was *tense*. Ten minutes down the road my youngest daughter, Remy, who is nine, said, "Mom, I need to go to the bathroom." Reading the "room," I whispered to her, "Sweetie, in this precarious moment, in this fragile state, I feel like the best thing for you to do is just pee your pants."

Honestly, half the time the road trip was a delight. The kids were cute, they were sweet, they were adorable. And I was thinking, *Look at this; this is precious. We're having a road trip like in the movies. This is amazing.* The other half of the time it was like a verbal assault from the back of the seat: "Stop touching me." "Stop looking at me." "Stop blinking." "Stop humming." "Stop breathing so loud." "Stop." "How much longer until we are going to get there?" "How many more miles is that?" "How many more minutes is that?" "I'm hungry." "I don't like this place." "I need to go to the bathroom." "Number 1." "Number 2." My husband puts in his headphones and acts like he's the only person in the car. So, what it sounds like is: "Mom, mom, mom!" "Mommy, mommy, mommy!"

During this opportunity for growth, those *eleven* hours in the car, I had the chance to go through what I call the Four Stages of Road Trip Management. (This may feel familiar to approximately everyone.)

PHASE ONE: PATIENT OPTIMISM. It's the first, say, three hours. There's a little bit of nurture to it, and so it kind of sounds like, "Children, let me help you work out this problem you're having so that we can come to an agreeable solution of which all of you will be satisfied." It's a little *Mary Poppins*.

PHASE TWO: IRRITATED INTERVENTION. Sometime between hours three and four I begin struggling to still care about their problems. And so the tone takes a turn. It starts to sound like, "You know what? Nobody in this car gets to *call* the seats. Do you know what I'm saying? I bought this car. I bought these seats. I get to *call* the seats. If you would like to call the seat, then you can get a job. Okay? Okay!"

PHASE THREE: TERRIFYING SERIAL KILLER MODE. It's probably around hour eight or nine that we hit phase three. It's that moment when you just sort of go dark. All the emotion drains out. You're basically dead inside. So it kind of sounds quiet and black like, "Listen children, new rule: From here on out, nobody may call me Mom. You just call me Jen. If I hear 'Mom' one more time inside the space of this vehicle, I will throw myself out of this moving car. And I will take at least two of you with me."

PHASE FOUR: QUIET ACCEPTANCE. For the last hour, y'all, you hit phase four. And honestly it is at this point that I become a five-point Calvinist. The kids are like, "When are we ever gonna get there?" And I'm like, "You know what? It's not for us to know. If it is God's will, we will get there when He predestined us to. Part of being a Christian means suffering."

Well, we actually got there. We arrived! Once we climbed out of the car, my attitude changed once more: *Oh, I like everyone again. Oh, that's right, I like you! I'm going to keep you all.*

Road trips for the win!

PRAYER FOR THIS WEEK . . .

Dear God, thank you that no matter what phase I'm in on my journey, you are right there in the car with me. As we travel this road together, help me to love my people well—even when they make me a little crazy.

LIKE A CHILD
Sarah Bessey

....

Keep on asking, and you will receive what you ask for.
Keep on seeking, and you will find.

MATTHEW 7:7

When we're sorting things out, when we dare ask questions, sometimes someone will pat us on the head and say, "Well, you know, you need to have faith like a child."

Pat, pat, pat right on the head. Patronise, patronise, patronise right on the soul. Just stop wondering, stop wrestling. You aren't supposed to be a grown-up in the kingdom, darling, you're supposed to be like a child and accept what you've been taught and stop asking questions. Trust the truth you've been given.

To which I now respectfully ask: I'm sorry, but have you ever been around a child for any amount of time?

Because let me tell you, kids ask a lot of questions.

My tinies ask questions constantly. They want to know

where the Eiffel Tower is and why it's there and why don't my friends go to church and why can't I marry Daddy and what time is it in China and what colors make pink and do you want to hear this song and why does this bug tickle me and why did Jesus die on the cross and why can't I watch this show and why do I need to sleep and on and on and ON.

There is a natural curiosity that is inherent to children.

I think it's a bit dishonest to use "Have faith like a child" as a way to shut a person down. Like, somehow, it means we're not supposed to wonder, we're just supposed to accept. Now that I have a house of small humanity, I think I'm beginning to understand why Jesus would encourage us to have faith like a child.

They don't know. *And so they ask.*

We don't know. And so we ask.

The asking isn't wrong. The wondering isn't wrong. The doubt isn't wrong. It's humbling to admit you don't know; it takes guts to ask and wrestle. The childlike quality isn't unthinking acquiescence: it's curiosity.

But here is the key of a child, the true wonder of child-like faith: They truly want to know. They're not asking to be cool or to push back on the establishment or to prove anyone wrong or to grind an ax or to make a point without making a change. Tinies ask because they want an answer.

So I'm in agreement with the words—have faith like a child—even if I'm not in agreement with the usual sentiment behind it.

Be curious. Look behind the curtain, push against the

answers, lean into the questions or the pain. As the psalmist wrote, fly on morning's wings to the far western horizon, God is already there.

God isn't threatened by our questions or our anger, our grief or our perplexed wonderings. I believe that the Spirit welcomes them, in fact, leads among them and in them. We ask because we want to know, because it matters to us, and so I believe it matters to God. And sometimes the answers are far wider and more welcoming than we ever imagined; other times our answer is to wait in the question, and sometimes the answer is another question altogether.

After all, in the Gospels, Jesus answered a lot of questions with more questions, pushing us to think in a new direction. It's interesting how often Jesus disrupted the comfortable— the ones who thought their answers were settled and done, the ones who were convinced that their righteousness was equal to their rightness. It's interesting how he poked and prodded, even how often he turned their answers around and moved them further into redemption than they were willing to go.

TO DO THIS WEEK . . .

Ask God some questions about things you want to know. You may be amazed at the answers you receive.

HOW TO SCREAM FOR HELP

Heather Kopp

I would always rather be happy than dignified.
CHARLOTTE BRONTË, *JANE EYRE*

I learned how to scream for help way before I learned to ask for it.

It happened one summer when my husband, Dave, and I were staying at a rental house on the Oregon coast. We just so happened to be in the bathroom at the same time—Dave in the shower and me drying my hair—when I heard a very loud crash. Alarmed, I tried to open the bathroom door to investigate. But it wouldn't budge.

"Honey?" I called to Dave, "I think we have a problem."

A half hour later, using a metal towel bar as a lever, we had finally managed to pry the upper part of the door open about an inch. Stuffing a towel in the crack to save our progress, we now had a narrow view of our predicament. A sliding door on the closet across from us had inexplicably escaped its track and fallen onto the bathroom door, jamming it shut. The more we tried to force the bath door open, the tighter the closet door wedged us in.

Naturally, this bathroom had no windows. Our cell phones were on the couch in the living room. None of our family or friends knew where we were. We could hardly believe it was happening. We were trapped? In a bathroom? The only contact we could count on was a cleaning lady who would come to clean after we checked out. In five days.

Trying to find humor in the situation, I pointed out to Dave that we had water, so we wouldn't die. And we'd lose a lot of weight. I had brought my *Oprah* magazine into the bathroom with me, so I settled on the toilet (lid down) and started reading aloud to Dave about how to live your best life.

Dave didn't think it was funny. Actually, he'd brought work along on vacation. How was he supposed to write devotionals about trusting God when he was stuck in a bathroom?

And then it hit me. My own big problem. By now, my alcoholism had progressed to the point where I drank copious amounts nightly just to feel normal (a third in front of Dave, the rest in secret, usually guzzled in the bathroom with the door locked. Oh, the irony!). Forget food—without a drink, I'd eventually go into withdrawal. Shakes. Sweating. I'd have to pretend to Dave that I had the flu.

Regalvanized by my private terror, I went back to the

crack in the door. This time, I realized that I could actually see into the bedroom down the hall. Dave had opened the window a few inches the night before. Even though it was rainy and windy, the people renting the house next door might hear us if we yelled loud enough.

Dave thought I should go first. "I think a woman's scream is louder and more alarming. People want to save a screaming woman."

I hesitantly put my face to the crack in the door and . . . I just couldn't do it. "Like, really loud?" I asked Dave, suddenly shy. "At the top of my lungs? But what do I say?"

"Try 'help,'" Dave said. "The loudest you can. Louder than you've ever screamed in your life."

It took me a while to work up to a *Psycho*-sized scream. I felt like an actress rehearsing for a horror movie. A few times, I started laughing. But soon I was letting loose with ear-piercing screams while Dave huddled in a corner, plugging his ears. When my throat got sore, I made him take a turn. But asking a grown man to scream for help is like asking him to run in the grocery store when you're at the register and realize you forgot something. It's beneath his dignity. He will only stroll.

Given that it was so hard on his pride, I won't even tell you that Dave can scream like a girl. We continued taking turns on and off for at least an hour. Then, my eye to the slit, I thought I saw a motion. A flash of yellow. The people next door were walking past our house! "You!" I screamed. "You in the yellow shirt! Help! You in the yellow! Help!"

The yellow stopped. It came toward the window, but slowly. Hesitant. I kept screaming. Finally, a woman's face peered in, and we were saved. As soon as she saw our predicament, this heavyset older lady shoved open the window and climbed through like a firefighter. It was dramatic and hilarious and something I never want to do again.

Recently someone asked me about recovery meetings. What were they really about? And why do I keep going if I don't drink anymore?

"It would take a while to explain," I started. And then I realized it was really very simple. "At first, we go there to ask for help," I told her. "And then we keep going so that when someone else asks for help, we're there to hear them."

There's more to it, to be sure. But asking for help is in some ways the main part, probably because it's the hardest part. When you remember that addiction is by nature an isolating phenomenon, it's no wonder the solution requires us to move in the opposite direction. For many of us, getting trapped by an addiction is our first experience of something we simply can't conquer on our own.

We're all but forced to learn how to yell for help.

Of course, even whispering, "I need help," or "I'm stuck and scared," or "I'm trapped by my obsession" is never easy. But in a way, that's the point. As soon as we give up hope that we can save ourselves from ourselves, as soon as we're willing to put down our pride and cry out for rescue, God shows up in a yellow shirt. And we are saved.

THOUGHT FOR THIS WEEK . . .

Do you need to call for help? Don't answer too quickly . . . think about it. Is there an area in your life where you're trying to save yourself—and failing? This week, if you determine that you need help, ask for it. Even if you have to scream.

ME, TOO

Melanie Dale

....

An honest answer is like a kiss of friendship.

PROVERBS 24:26

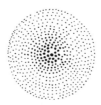

Sitting in the sunshine watching our kiddos dig in the dirt, my friend shares about struggling with anxiety, that heart-pounding, clenching, can't breathe, suffocating stress. As the words bubble out of her, I nod, murmuring, "Me, too."

She sighs. "Really? So it's not just me?"

At a restaurant with another adoptive mom, over a steaming plate of chicken tikka masala, I choke out my deepest fear about parenting, the underlying knife hovering by my heart as we struggle with attachment and forging this adoption bond after brokenness. "The thing I fear the most is what if she rejects God as she rejects me?"

She whispers, "Me, too. I worry about that, too."

In his room crumpled on the carpet, my son sobs to me, "Sometimes I just get so mad and I make bad choices, Mommy!"

"Me, too, sweetheart. Me, too." He blinks back tears and looks up at me. I watch as despair drains from his face and something like hope crinkles the side of his mouth.

On the phone with a friend worrying that the daily toil of marriage is too exhausting, "Sometimes I feel like I want to give up and stop working so hard." "Me, too."

Me, too. These may be the two most powerful words in a relationship.

Nothing brings a bigger sigh of relief than knowing that someone understands, that we're not crazy, that we're not beyond hope.

I often feel just a little bit messier than everyone else, just a little less together, like everyone is a bit shinier than I am, a tad closer to nailing it. When one of these shiny people enters into my overly honest ramblings and offers "Me, too," I realize we're all just people, whether our clothes are ironed and our beds are made, or we live on the wrinkly side of life.

I love these friends, the ones who enter in, who choose to accept my invitation to honest relationship. Here's my hurt, here's my fear, here's my kitchen with the oatmeal bowl from yesterday. Are you ready to show me yours?

Please don't wash my bowl. Don't fix my fear. But please, if you can, share a "Me, too."

I want to be a "Me, too" friend. I want to be a "Me, too" mom and wife. A safe place where people can share their fears and struggles and find refuge and empathy, rather than pity or shame.

Maybe our issues are a little bit different, but we can enter into the sacred space of shared feelings and pain.

We're on the same team. You're not alone. We both struggle, and we can struggle together.

Are you praying for something and scared that God might not answer the way you want Him to? Me, too.

Are you worried you're messing up your kids? Me, too.

Are you still in your jammies as you read this? Me, too.

I've been reading through the book of John, and a few days ago I read John 8, when the crowd brings the woman "caught" in adultery to Jesus to stone her and he says something like, "Let he who is without sin throw the first stone." One by one, as they each drop their stones on the ground and walk away, they are really saying, "Me, too. I'm a sinner, too." Me, too. Me, too. Me, too.

There's commonality in the ways that we fear, and there's commonality in the ways that we fail, and when we partner in the pain, it gives way to sharing in the joy as well.

From the pit of despair to the pinnacle of triumph, I am so glad we have each other on this difficult, dazzling, unexpected ride.

PRAYER FOR THIS WEEK . . .

Dear God, thank you that I'm not the only one. Show me others who can relate to what I'm going through and help me to be a "Me, too" person for the people around me.

LEADING WITH OUR SERVE

Patricia Raybon

....

But among you it will be different. Whoever wants to be
a leader among you must be your servant.

MATTHEW 20:26

We're standing in the kitchen, watching Serena Williams blast through the final set of the Miami Open tournament.

"It's her serve," says my husband.

I nod, but feel confused. "We're watching tennis?"

We'd been surfing channels for an NCAA basketball championship game, the "real" sports competition on this particular weekend.

But first, here is Serena Williams. Leading in our kitchen without apology.

"Watch her serve," my husband says, putting down the remote to watch the tennis champ's final set.

Dan is a longtime tennis fan, even though he hasn't played

in years, not since emergency brain surgery in 2000 compromised his body balance. Still, he follows the game.

"*Another* ace," Dan says, admiring Serena's court precision. "That's how you win at tennis."

The TV announcer is saying the same thing. "Watch her placement."

Sure enough, Serena, at age thirty-three, is conducting a service clinic on her opponent, twenty-six-year-old Carla Suarez Navarro of Spain, the twelfth seed.

"Despite her age," whispers the announcer about Williams, "Serena is simply a student of the game."

Indeed, with this match—which she won in fifty-six minutes 6–2, 6–0—Williams becomes only the fourth woman after Martina Navratilova, Steffi Graf, and Chris Evert to win the same WTA tournament at least eight times.

It's her serve. And the metaphor is obvious.

Yet it's worth noting, because the road to success—whether in tennis, leadership, ministry, relationships, or life—is never easy.

Williams, for example, was so "viciously" booed and trash-talked by fans of her semifinal opponent the night before that *USA Today* writer Chris Chase wrote an editorial to denounce their behavior.[1]

Still Williams won. Game. Set. Match. How? She leads on service. Yep, that metaphor again.

In our service to others, our focus, passion, endurance, and commitment to delivery determines our outcome.

In short, we don't run all over the court to make our mark. We just serve. Well.

Jesus, indeed, on the night he was betrayed, wrapped a towel around his waist to demonstrate this essential and holy principle.

He washed his disciples' feet. Then he went to the cross— scourged, trash-talked, and ridiculed. Still he saved the world.

And his leadership is eternal. But how did it start? With dirty feet. And a Savior willing to wash them.

Now what about us?

PRAYER FOR THIS WEEK . . .

Lord, help me see opportunities to serve in the days ahead. Give me the grace to do so with an open heart and willing hands.

THE TRUTH ABOUT PERFECTIONISM

Alli Worthington

Give the best you have, and it will never be enough.
Give your best anyway.

MOTHER TERESA

Perfectionism is not excellence; it is procrastination based in fear.

What are you waiting for?

Are you waiting for the time to be right?

Are you waiting for the moment you feel you have all of the puzzle pieces?

Are you waiting for the phase when you have enough uninterrupted time?

Are you waiting until you feel like it?

Or are you going to keep waiting, all the while feeling bad about not doing anything?

When you chase perfection, you set yourself up for

disappointment, and all too easily it is used as a form of procrastination. There will never be a perfect moment when you feel completely ready.

No one feels completely capable or has unlimited funds, time, and energy to achieve his or her goals. And everyone is terrified of failure, looking foolish, and letting others down.

It's not about waiting for the time to be right. It's about taking action because your vision is worth it.

SEVEN WAYS TO CURB PERFECTIONISM

1. **DO SOMETHING.** And if it is not perfect, focus on the fact that you actually took action. The crucial step in breaking the cycle of perfectionism is to simply start doing things and be gentle with yourself in the process.

2. **REEXAMINE YOUR STANDARDS.** My guess is that you are overly critical of yourself. Do this exercise often: Pretend your friend is asking your opinion about his performance at a certain task or her project results. What would you say? I bet if your results or performance were the same as someone else's, you would not be so critical.

3. **LOOK AT THE BIG PICTURE.** Ask yourself if what you're worried about really matters. Will it matter next week, next month, next year? Probably not. So criticizing yourself over the situation won't help you either.

This is also a great way to look at tasks and judge if they are important. Because we want things done perfectly, even small tasks that aren't important can get treated like critical matters we must attend to. Ask yourself, "Is this really that important?" If not, let it slide.

4. **SHARE YOUR WORKS IN PROGRESS.** Yep, that's right. Share the drafts that have mistakes and typos, just make sure they say DRAFT. Consider this to be therapy that will help you fight the urge to make everything perfect before anyone sees it.

Not long ago, a draft version of a blog post I wrote was published. It was full of typos and unfinished sentences—and I didn't notice for hours. Guess what? It's over. I survived and it doesn't matter. I had to just let it slide.

5. **SET MORE REALISTIC GOALS.** Rather than encouraging my clients to set the goal of "I will write a *New York Times* bestseller" and then watching them be overwhelmed by the big dream and freezing up, I work with them to break down their goal into manageable steps.

When looking at your big dreams, reverse engineer them and define what you need to do at each stage to achieve your goals.

6. **BREAK THE ADDICTION OF COMPARING YOURSELF TO OTHERS.** From a psychological standpoint, people compare their lives to those of others, leading to unhappiness, jealousy, and envy. Dan Ariely describes this in his book *Predictably Irrational*: "the more we have, the more we want."[2] Instead of focusing on the success and seemingly perfect life of someone else, focus on what gives you joy, what you feel proud of, and what makes you feel content in your work.

    Side note: This is yet another reason to stay off Facebook. Don't compare your real life to anyone else's curated image of life.

7. **DO A GUT CHECK.** Ask yourself daily: *Am I striving for excellence or demanding perfection?* Excellence is a worthy goal that energizes and inspires; perfectionism wraps us in guilt and ends progress. #PerfectionismLies

Ending the cycle of being unreasonably hard on yourself is a process. . . . Now, take a deep breath and start taking action. Every masterpiece started out messy.

TO DO THIS WEEK . . .

Do something! You might start with putting Alli's "Seven Ways to Curb Perfectionism" into practice, but don't stop there. Your masterpiece is waiting for you to begin.

GETTING LOST, STAYING FOUND
Nichole Nordeman

See, I have written your name on the palms of my hands.
ISAIAH 49:16

I was piling the kids into the car to pick up friends from the airport, running predictably and woefully behind schedule. Winding my way out of our wooded, hilly neighborhood, I was trying to make a conscious effort not to let my speed limit reflect my heart rate. On this particular day, my self-restraint served me well because as I came over the last blind hill, I hit the brakes just in front of a furry little lump sitting smack in the center of the road.

Peering through the windshield, I saw, upon closer examination, that this lump had a really wiggly tail and a tiny, wet pink tongue. He was trembling and, I think, peeing on himself. His coat was matted and tangled, and he was staring up at me with a reluctant hope peeking out of the one eye that wasn't swollen shut.

Not today. Not today. Not todaaay, I begged. This is the universal prayer of animal lovers everywhere who are incapable of looking the other way. We have no choice in the matter.

I stopped, of course. Picked up the trembling lump. Texted Shannon that we would be a few (more) minutes late getting to the airport. And then we headed back to the house. We promised we'd be right back. The poor pup passed out from exhaustion before we'd even shut the door. I spent the rest of the drive to the airport and back trying to talk my son out of giving him a name. Too late. Charlie had already named him Rex.

With his name enthusiastically agreed upon, Rex limped his way into our hearts in about a minute and a half. His eye was pretty messed up. So I spent that afternoon at the vet's office getting treatment and meds, insisting he wasn't a permanent family addition.

The kids were delirious with joy in his lumpy little presence. I insisted he wasn't ours, trying to help them imagine how sad another family might be right now. I had to at least *try*, so after checking lost-and-found websites galore, I finally made some posters. Shannon stayed home with Rex and the kids while I dashed out to post copies, but in my heart I was secretly hoping we were the proud owners of a new (although slightly damaged) Yorkie.

I slowed down at the very first intersection, armed with a roll of tape and a stack of posters, and right away spied a little boy about Charlie's age next to his mom, taping up his own poster to a telephone pole.

MISSING:
YORKIE WITH A HURT EYE.
MY BEST FRIEND.
PLEASE CALL US IF YOU SEE HIM.

I pressed my palm into my chest and winced. I approached them slowly with a determined smile, warmed at the sight of this sweet little guy still in his pajama pants, high on tippy toes, handing his mom pieces of torn tape. I recognized her agony, too, the bags beneath her eyes, the forced hopeful, chipper tone. When I told them we had Rex, the boy literally collapsed to his knees bawling. Then his mom started. And just to be a team player, so did I. I couldn't believe how I found Rex in such close proximity to where he actually went missing. Just a few streets over. He looked like he'd been hitchhiking for months.

They followed me on the short drive back to our house to reclaim their pup, where more tears awaited us. A different kind.

To her credit, the mother recognized what this moment was costing us. She delayed her own celebration and instead bent down to tell Charlie what an answer to prayer he was. How they had prayed so hard that their dog would be safe with a loving family and God had used us to answer that prayer. Her sensitivity didn't mean much to Charlie, but it meant the world to me.

As they were preparing to go, one of us asked what Rex's real name was. I honestly don't remember their answer. I do remember thinking that it didn't fit him at all. But sure enough, as soon as they said it, his tail started wagging at record speeds. He had tolerated us calling him Rex, but he certainly knew his real name. And he knew who he belonged to.

I thought about how critical it is to really know your own name despite anyone else's efforts to reprogram you. I find myself circling back to the importance of my own name. God gave me several of them, actually. *Nichole. Child of God. Beloved. Ransomed. Daughter. Forgiven. Seeker. Finder.*

It's when I find myself stuck in the middle of a road, lost, hungry, and exhausted, flea-infested, and looking at the world through my one good eye that I start answering to other names. *Failure. Prodigal. Naive. Arrogant. Neurotic. Insecure. Angry. Nervous. Desperate. Hopeless.* And after being scooped up and rescued, cleaned and cared for, after a good meal and a long nap in the safe arms of the One who knows me and named me, it is only then I realize how close I was to home all along. Just a few streets over. My heart just forgot.

PRAYER FOR THIS WEEK . . .

Dear Lord, sometimes I feel just like Rex—lost, damaged, and alone. Help me remember that I'm never far from the place I belong—safe in your arms. If you send other "lost pups" my way this week, I'll try to show them the way home to you.

HIDE YOUR SCARS?

Amy Potts

A while back as I was visiting with an acquaintance, she noticed two scars on my arm from a couple of surgeries. She inquired about them, and after a bit of conversation, she said, "You really should keep those covered." When I asked why, she said, "Because they bother me and they probably bother other people too."

Initially I was angry at the suggestion and then perhaps self-conscious about how my arm must appear to others. But should I wear long sleeves in the heat of summer just to spare someone the appearance of a couple of scars? (Not many people notice the scars, and those who do aren't usually distracted by them.)

I see and feel my scars every single day; they remind me of a day that will *not* be listed as one of my favorite days. I will, in time, forget about that day—until someone asks me again about the scars. It will be okay then, and the explanation will be short and simple because as time goes by, the details will be less and less important. At least that is how I suppose it will be.

We all have scars from childhood nicks and scrapes; maybe even a long scar left from an open-heart surgery. Some scars are visible; others are kept hidden out of embarrassment. Then there are the scars of inner wounds: griefs that never quite heal, memories that cannot be erased, hurtful words that still cause us to well up with tears when we recall them. All of us have been scarred in one way or another. You can't get through life without scars, inside or outside.

In the Bible, John tells the story of Jesus' appearance to his disciples after the Resurrection (John 20:19-31). He explains how Jesus showed them his scars—not once, but twice.

Thomas, who wasn't among the disciples for Jesus' first appearance, was, in fact, a little tardy to the party. The other disciples told him about Jesus' visible scars, but Thomas was a bit skeptical. "Unless I see the nail marks in his hands and put my finger where the nails were, and put my hand into his side, I will not believe" (NIV).

A week later, Jesus came to the disciples again. This time Thomas was there with them. So Jesus took away his doubts. "Put your finger here," he said, holding out his hands to Thomas. We don't know for sure if Thomas did what Jesus invited him to do. We are told that Thomas fell to his knees. Whether it was the sight of Jesus alive or the sight of the wounds that brought Thomas to his knees in recognition and adoration, we don't know.

Why did Jesus show the disciples his wounds? Why did his resurrected body even have wounds? Wouldn't it make more sense to show himself in a new body, sleek and whole, marking his complete victory over sin and death? I'm not sure of the answer to those questions. But if Jesus had not had scars when he was resurrected, I don't know that Thomas would have believed that he was who he said he was.

The wounded Christ is the Savior of a wounded community. There's scar tissue all over the place: Some of it is visible, while some hides beneath the surface. But sometimes we walk around as if we are above life's mess. Whether we cover our scars with long sleeves or not, we aren't fooling anyone. And really, if our wounds are hidden from the community, no one may believe that Jesus is who he says he is. It's often wounded, broken, forgiven people who point others to Jesus.

It's okay for people to see our scars. In fact, being able to see our wounds might be what makes us real. A dear friend gave me the children's book *The Velveteen Rabbit* by Margery Williams at a very difficult time in my life. In this beautiful story, a wise, old toy horse tells the stuffed rabbit, "Generally, by the time you are Real, most of your hair has been loved off, and your eyes drop out and you get loose in the joints and very shabby. But these things don't matter at all, because once you are Real you can't be ugly, except to people who don't understand."

Our wounds, whether internal or not, may be the very thing to help someone see that you are who you say you are—and that the God who has brought healing to your life is who he says he is.

Don't hide your scars. . . .

THOUGHT FOR THIS WEEK . . .

Have you been hiding scars? What has kept you from sharing them? What's the worst thing that could happen if you let your scars see the light of day? What's the best thing that could come from authentically sharing your wounds? You don't need to splash them across the Internet or gab about them on a television talk show. Think about it, pray about it, and ask God to show you when, where, and how to take the first step.

PRIDE

Kathleen Norris

....

When pride comes, then comes shame;
but with the humble is wisdom.

PROVERBS 11:2, NKJV

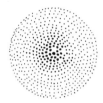

The young monk read from the Bible: "The Lord God called to the man, and said to him, 'Where are you?' He said, 'I heard the sound of you in the garden, and I was afraid, because I was naked; and I hid myself.'" I have always found that to be a poignant summary of the human response to evil: I was afraid, I tried to hide.

I thought I knew where I was, at an everyday monastery Mass. But I was distracted for a moment by a thought that seemed absurdly out of place; I recalled that I'd forgotten to put on my favorite silver bracelet, the one I usually wear. It was handmade by the husband of an old friend, who gave it to me when I graduated from college. In the crazed atmosphere of Bennington in the 1960s, when so many faculty were having affairs with students that it was easy to become cynical about marriage, this couple had always seemed remarkably stable to me, still in love after more than twenty years, and good to be with.

I tried to concentrate on the gospel reading, a peculiar one: After Jesus began to preach, to cast out demons and heal the sick, some people had assumed that he'd gone mad. They tried to convince his family that Jesus himself was possessed by demons and should be restrained. "How do we respond to the good?" the monk asked in his homily. "How do we respond to the presence of the good?"

Suddenly I remembered another silver bracelet, lost in the shadows of my life, one my husband had given me, or had tried to give me, years before. It was beautiful lying in its box, but I was disappointed to find that it was a cuff bracelet, a kind I've never liked to wear. I had suggested to David that we replace it, or ask the silversmith, the woman who'd made his wedding band, if she could modify it. He said that he would, but I never heard any more about it. Now, for some reason, I remembered this event, and saw it clearly for the first time. The gift was good, and I had rejected it. I know my husband well enough to know that he would have taken it as a rejection and also that most likely he still had the bracelet buried among his things. I resolved to ask him, and also to apologize.

David was surprised, but he did remember, and after a few days found the bracelet in its original box. He polished it, and I now wear it. And all because I heard two questions: "Where are you?" and "How do we respond to the good?"

The other reading at Mass that day was from Paul's second letter to the Corinthians: "We do not lose heart . . . our inner being is being renewed every day." My pride will resist any change I haven't chosen, but it's powerless against this force of which Paul speaks, the conversion that occurs without my even being aware of it, except when it erupts suddenly into my life. A statement of John Climacus, typically self-contained and bristling with certitude, suddenly made sense to me: "Men can heal the lustful. Angels can heal the malicious. Only God can heal the proud."

PRAYER FOR THIS WEEK . . .

God, I want to "respond to the good" in a good way, in the way you would have me respond. Let me not be afraid to answer when you ask, "Where are you?" Help me identify any areas in my heart where pride is clouding my judgment and leading me to cause pain to those around me.

WHEN YOU AREN'T SURE WHAT YOU'RE SUPPOSED TO DO NEXT

Natalie Snapp

....

*And the LORD said to me, "I have seen this people,
and they are a stiff-necked people indeed!"*

DEUTERONOMY 9:13, NIV

I have this habit of sharing my heart on my Facebook page.

I don't always mean to do so. It's just that sometimes I sit down and there's the status update box, looking me straight in the eye.

It *asks* me what's on my mind, after all.

Well, Facebook . . . if you really must know . . . I'm kind of in this spot where I wonder, *What do I do next?*

I mean, I know what writing project I'm doing next, but I'm thinking even past that because my heart longs to write some stuff that others "in the know" don't think will sell.

So then I get frustrated because it's a very loud world. So much is being said these days that I wonder if I even need to add to the words.

Then I wonder if I should go back to school and get my MA in counseling (on the radar).

Then I wonder if I should just be a wife and mom. Yes. *Just.* Ha. Ha. Ha.

Then I wonder why on earth I don't have this figured out yet. I'm forty-two years old, for crying out loud.

So as I was lamenting all this to God (yes, I already prayed for the horrible situations going on in the world), I asked Him to give me some confirmation as to what path He wants me to take because I'm just so utterly confused.

As soon as the words were off my lips, I laughed because I remember wondering how many signs the Israelites were going to ask God to provide while they were wandering in the desert after being rescued from slavery in Egypt. (You'll find the whole story in the Bible's Old Testament, mostly in Exodus.)

God said of them, "They are a stiff-necked people."

And so often, I read about them and I think, *Goodness gracious, people. He just freaking delivered you out of slavery, for the love. Is it never enough? Are we that self-absorbed?*

Lovely judgment. I know.

Because the thing is . . . I am no different from the Israelites.

I want something to eat other than the manna God provides. I want to know where I'm going. I want water when I want water. I don't want to go the long way.

I mean, really. Come. On. God.

Yes, indeed. Stiff-necked I am. (And apparently, I also talk like Yoda now and then.)

I don't know what God wants me to do next. I'm guessing you've felt that way a time or two as well.

But maybe what He wants us to do is this:

Be present in the now. Look at the manna He's already given us. Trust that He really will light our paths. Drink from the living water when we're thirsty. Appreciate the process of the long way rather than the quickness of the short way.

Yep. Just maybe that's what we're supposed to do.

TO DO THIS WEEK . . .

Purpose to be present this week: Focus on what is rather than what may come. Look around and admire the view from this stage of your life. If you spot a rose, take a moment to enjoy its scent. Your future will still arrive in its time, and you'll enjoy the journey so much more.

THROWING CANDY
Shauna Niequist

Attitude is a little thing that makes a big difference.

UNKNOWN

I had an experience a couple of summers ago that changed everything for me. That sounds hyperbolic, I know. But every once in a while we have these experiences that slice our lives into *before* and *after,* and this was one of those for me.

A friend of a friend invited me on a trip to a place I'd never been with a group of people, most of whom I'd never met. I didn't know what to expect, but I did have this sense that there was something waiting for me there—something I needed to learn. A conversation, a lesson, a moment.

There was lots of space and silence. The stars were so bright, and the layers and layers of stress and regret and toughness I'd been wearing for ages slipped off one by one, like an armor, until there I was, just me.

And without that armor, it's like I could feel everything and see everything with such clarity. It was like Technicolor, and I knew that there was something there for me to see. I could sense it. For the first time in a long time, I was really paying attention.

One of the traditions of this place where we were gathered is that when you see kayakers, no matter what you're doing, you stop and you throw candy to them. Because it's fun. Because it's a sweet tradition. Because it makes people happy.

If you knew me ten years ago, you'd say that kind of thing is *so Shauna*. She's totally the candy-throwing type. But to be totally honest, I don't know if you'd say that about me the last couple of years.

One afternoon, the kayakers crossed in front of our dock while about a million other things were happening. Two large power boats were docking, as well as a sailboat, and a few paddle boarders were trying not to get in the way. There were swimmers in the water. It was all happening right at the same time, in a relatively small space.

But the man who was in charge of it all, our host, the one who owned all the stuff that was about to crash in a thousand ways, stopped what he was doing and sprinted down the dock to get the lollipops.

I had a little panic attack because what he was doing seemed so irresponsible (*warning word: irresponsible*). He threw candy, right in the middle of it. Everything swirled around him, and he kept throwing candy, over and over, handful after handful.

And everything was fine. All the boats were docked safely, nothing happened.

As I watched from the deck of the lodge, I put my head down on the wide railing, and I began to sob.

Because I used to throw candy, right in the middle of it all. I used to throw candy no matter what. I used to be warm and whimsical. I used to believe in the power of silliness and memory making and laughter.

And then I became the kind of person who threw candy as long as nothing else was going on—as long as it didn't get in the way of being responsible. I threw candy at approved and sanctioned candy-throwing time, after all the work was done and things were safe and lunches were made.

And then I got so wrapped up in being responsible that there was never time to throw candy.

And then, from the world I created for myself, a world of should and hustle and frantic, I looked over at the candy throwers and thought *Must be nice.* Must be nice to have the luxury of being so irresponsible.

Must be nice is a warning sign. It can point us to the things we're longing for, if we're honest with ourselves. *Must be nice* to be present and connected and fun.

You know what? It is. It is nice to be connected and present and fun. It's more than nice. It's life changing. It's the ball game.

Those are the hardest changes I've made in a long time. And they're the most valuable. I'm never going back.

I'm done with that kind of responsible. I don't want to get to the end of my life and look back and realize that the best thing about me was that I was organized. That I executed well, that I ran a tight ship, that I never missed a detail. That's not living. I want to look back and remember all the times I threw candy, even when it didn't make sense. *Especially* when it didn't make sense.

I know how hard it is to juggle everything. I'm in it, with little kids and a full-time job and dreams for the future and regrets about the past.

I'm in it. And I'm throwing candy every chance I get.

PRAYER FOR THIS WEEK . . .

Dear God, I don't want to stand on the deck thinking, "Must be nice" while missing out on all the fun. I want to be someone who takes advantage of every candy-throwing opportunity you give me—and who helps those around me enjoy the candy, too. Help me to be connected and present and fun. Just like you.

BRINGING THE FISH

Kelly O'Dell Stanley

....

*"There's a young boy here with five barley loaves and two fish.
But what good is that with this huge crowd?"*

JOHN 6:9

One day Jesus fed 4,000 people with seven loaves and a few fish, and another time He fed 5,000 from just five loaves and two fish.

The beauty of these stories is the point that God is not limited in His ability to provide. He always brings more than enough. There is always increase when God is involved. And there are always leftovers.

Knowing this story, though, doesn't necessarily make believing it any easier. No matter how strong you think your faith is, you will have times when you doubt. When you wonder if what God gives you will really be enough. If God will intervene in time (or at all). You might be thinking, *Maybe somehow I'm exempt. Maybe I don't deserve it. Maybe He's too busy to notice. Maybe this is too trivial to bother God with.*

And the heart of our deepest fears: *Maybe He doesn't care.*

If you always knew the outcome, you wouldn't need faith. If you've been fortunate enough to notice God's provision in the past, it's a little easier to hold on, whether He came through for you or for someone else—because, in theory, you have seen with your own eyes that it's possible. But even if you think you believe with your whole heart, the skeptic inside your brain may be shouting, as mine does, *Wait! Hold on a second! How in the world do I get there from here? How do I make the leap to thousands of loaves when all I have in front of me are a few crumbs?*

Guess what? You don't have to. The answer lies not in what you have in front of you, but what God has in front of Him. Before Jesus worked miracles, He took stock of what He had to work with, what was really there. Which brings us to the often-overlooked, and in my opinion, most critical fact in this story: *Someone had to provide the fish.*

The young boy who offered his lunch didn't create the miracle. God could have done it without him. I believe God regularly creates something from nothing—a faithful loving marriage where there was formerly no trust. Peace in the midst of black-clothed mourners at a funeral. More often, He works with what we initially bring to Him, with what we stretch forward in our hands as an offering, whether literally or symbolically.

The more we're willing to let go of, the more He multiplies. We plant a seed of giving by paying tithes and offerings and donating to charitable organizations. When we put aside our egos and desires, we make room for His presence. To see God accomplish above and beyond that which we can even imagine, we must first offer Him our whole selves— bodies, hearts, minds, and souls—and mean it when we ask Him to use us. Because when we do, God *will* multiply. He *will* create. He *will* increase—starting with exactly what you offered Him. Don't ever fall into the trap of believing that God won't come through because of your current (or past) failings. Or that what you have to offer isn't enough. He's already given you everything you need to see Him, to find Him, to reach Him.

Stand tall and open your hands. Speak toward the heavens: *Lord, I may not have much, but I offer You my fish. Multiply this offering. I believe. . . .*

Here's the funny thing about God: He rarely draws our answers in straight lines. Yet the answers still come. His solutions often seem convoluted, confusing, maybe even down-to-the-last-second crazy. We cling to stories of miraculous solutions. The check (or tax refund or bonus or raise) arrives the day the bill you thought you couldn't pay is due. Doctors mention terrifying words like *aneurysm* and *cancer* and *inoperable*, so you have the tests done and pray, and suddenly, although the doctors can't explain it, the condition is gone or the symptoms weren't what they seemed. We lose a job and panic, worried about how to provide for our families, but then another, better opportunity presents itself and we wonder why we didn't leave the old job sooner. God always delivers—somehow, some way.

On the other hand, it's disappointing, sometimes devastating, when His answer isn't the one you'd hoped for—when the cancer comes back, or your spouse doesn't return home—or when His timing doesn't match yours. God's ways are not our ways . . .

> "My thoughts are nothing like your thoughts," says
> the LORD.
> "And my ways are far beyond anything you could
> imagine.
> For just as the heavens are higher than the earth,
> so my ways are higher than your ways
> and my thoughts higher than your thoughts."
> ISAIAH 55:8-9

Some answers may thrill your soul, and others may break your heart. He knows what He's doing, even if we can't see it yet. Even if we can't fathom that any good could possibly exist in the midst of suffering or sorrow, it does. God sees that what is tragic or heartbreaking—what feels like the end to us—really is not the end of the story. He promises He "will never leave you nor forsake you," which means He will always stay beside you as you face whatever comes your way.

Because He is *always* in the answer. And He doesn't make mistakes.

PRAYER FOR THIS WEEK . . .

Dear God, what I have to offer seems so insignificant—but then, so did that little boy's lunch compared to a hungry crowd of thousands, and I see what You did with that. So here's my "fish" for you to do with as you will. Help me remember that whatever you do with my offering, You know what is best for me.

WHO AM I *NOW*?

September Vaudrey

*Suffering will change you—but not necessarily for the better.
You have to choose that.*

WAYNE CORDEIRO

The year that my nineteen-year-old daughter died was—as you can imagine—a year I wouldn't care to repeat. Katie was driving to her first day of her summer job when an aneurysm ruptured in her brain. Then came the car accident, the "your daughter is brain-dead," the organ-donation surgery, the funeral—and then she was gone, and our family's world was forever changed. My husband and I, and our four remaining kids (ages fourteen to twenty-three) were devastated. The "anything but that" nightmare had become my reality.

In those early weeks and months after the funeral, the weight of grief was almost unbearable. One afternoon, I needed to be alone, so I stepped into our backyard to feel all the horrid feelings and cry what I needed to cry. I lay down on the grass, closed my eyes, and gazed into the horizon of my Katieless future. *Is my life ruined? Am I disqualified from God's plans for me? Am I simply to take up permanent residence on the injured reserve bench of life?* Everything had changed, and it terrified me. *Who am I?* Or rather, *Who am I now?*

Before that fateful day, I could have answered the "Who am I?" question with ease: I am a Christ follower, wife, and Mother of Five. I was proud of our lively, well-behaved gaggle of kids. Not many families these days have five or more children, and I secretly liked belonging to this elite group. Mostly, I loved our family's close-knit community of seven.

But now, people viewed me not as Mother of Five, but as Mother Whose Child Died. In an instant, my twenty-three years of raising a large family were eclipsed by a more dramatic story: the loss of a child. I wanted my old life back. I had loved my identity as Mother of Five—but Katie was gone, and like it or not, I was now a child-loss parent, a member of the Grief Club. I was Mother Whose Child Died.

I've met a number of people whose stories, like mine, include significant losses—death, divorce, shattered dreams. A few seem resigned to their tragedies, acquiescing to bitterness or self-pity or victimhood. This could so easily become me: I fear my daughter will be forgotten and—if I'm totally honest—that people will forget my pain. As I lay there in our yard, I felt the allure of letting Katie's death swallow me whole.

But others—people whose losses equal or surpass mine—have come out the other side more alive, more joyful, and more filled with a deep, gentle wisdom. They tell me they have leaned into their pain rather than away from it, grieving wholeheartedly and allowing the fertile soil of sorrow to do its transforming work in their souls. I wanted to become like those people. But how?

Lying there in the grass, an image formed in my mind: a trail meandering through a dense stretch of woods—peaceful, beautiful, serene. But suddenly in my mind's eye, a giant boulder came crashing into view, smashing the trail and leaving a gaping crater in its wake before continuing on its way.

My life was that trail, and Katie's death was the boulder. The path to the future as I'd planned it was destroyed, and the crater left behind was too wide to go around. The only way forward was through.

As I lay there, warm tears slipping from my eyes, I sensed a whisper from God. *You didn't have a choice with this boulder—you couldn't have stopped it—but you can fill that crater it left behind. You have full control. You get to decide. What will you put in that crater?*

I had a choice. What would I fill my crater with? I could think of all kinds of things that would fit nicely: bitterness, doubt, anger. No one would judge me if I chose those things.

I drifted back to that question, *Who am I* now? I had been confusing identity with role. I am both Mother Whose Child Died and Mother of Five, but these are just roles based on circumstance. Neither is my identity.

Roles may shift, but *our circumstances are not the boss of us.* They can't ruin our lives without our permission. My identity, on the other hand, is unchanging, proclaimed by my Good Father from the beginning of time: I am His child. He loves me, and His goodness trumps my pain at every turn.

Each day, as I stand on the precipice of my crater, I face a decision. Each day I get to choose to invite grief and joy, sorrow and laughter, light and love into the gaping hole that Katie's death created in my soul.

THOUGHT FOR THIS WEEK . . .

What circumstance has left a crater in your soul? What are you filling your crater with? What step can you take this week to grieve your loss—and invite sorrow to do its transforming work in you?

A FAMILY CRISIS MANIFESTO

Jen Hatmaker

To cheer one on the tedious way, to fetch one if one goes astray,
to lift one if one totters down, to strengthen whilst one stands.

CHRISTINA ROSSETTI

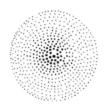

As adult children, when one of your parents gets sick, everyone reverts to their standard roles. So five hours before my mom's breast cancer surgery, some of us prayed, some assembled snacks, some set up a care calendar. *I wrote an essay.* (I am a firstborn, controlling, career writer; I had no alternative.) I believe these guidelines apply to any family in crisis and those who love them:

THE KING FAMILY CANCER MANIFESTO

Mom goes in for surgery in five hours. Obviously, we hope the surgery will be the end of this, and Mom will kick cancer's tail, and we'll get back to our important issues like

Lindsay's grilled pimento cheese recipe for her new menu and
. . . whatever it is Dad does at the ranch.

Amy H. gave me this idea she read in the *LA Times*.[3] It
goes like this:

- We have concentric rings around Mom's cancer, and
  she gets to be in the bulls-eye, because, well, she has
  the actual cancer.
- The first ring is Dad, because he said "in sickness and
  in health" forty-five years ago and so now he is stuck.
- Us four kids are second, because we are the fruit of
  their loins (gross).
- The people we married or "are hanging out with" or
  birthed are in the next ring, because Mom is their
  Grana or mother-in-law or "mom of the guy she is
  hanging out with."
- The fourth ring includes all our best friends. The real
  ones. The ones we ask to help us move and crap like
  that. The ones who walk into our houses without
  knocking.
- The outer ring includes our work friends and church
  friends and neighbors who like or even love us, and
  they will get swept into our cancer vortex by proximity.
- Everyone else in the world is outside of those rings.

The way this works is that stress can always go out but never
in. *Mom is in the bulls-eye, so she can say and do and feel whatever
she wants at all times.* No other rings can dump their worry, fear,

or burdens on Mom. She is the Cancer Queen and zero drama can reach her on the throne. We have to be strong and steady at all times for Mom. I don't know how we'll manage, as this is not our skill set. Maybe there is a YouTube tutorial.

Dad is next. He can't give Mom any fuss ever, but he can give it to anyone outside his ring. We have to absorb Dad's junk too. Dad gets to say all the words in all the world and everyone outside his ring has to listen patiently, because the only person who gets to shut him down ever is Mom.

The family is next, so none of our crazy can go in toward Mom or Dad, but it can absolutely go out to the other rings. Our best friends are the recipients of all melodrama, inflated enthusiasm, and emotional outbursts. They can give us exactly zero of those things. Outer rings can only send in the good. Absolutely no crazy. Crazy-senders get booted from the rings immediately.

If people outside our rings want to help, they can pray. Remember? We believe in God! We know God loves Mom, and if we are not one of His favorite families, then God has no taste at all. *He's got us. I know it.*

So no matter what comes later today and next week and this whole next year, we can handle this. We have each other and we have God and we have good rings. We can do this.

•   •   •

On this side of the manifesto, I can tell you that the ring system *works*. If the rings are maintained well, the bulls-eye person gets to sit in a soothing emotional spa of calm and serenity and love. Good outer rings constantly strengthen the inner rings.

For my mom, this looked like a stocked refrigerator for weeks, an unusually calm family, gifts for every single day of radiation from her staff, a cleaned house, rotating hand-holders on radiation days at the oncology office, anointing her with oil and prayer, baskets of lotion, tons of e-mails and texts.

For us in the innermost rings, this looked like a billion calls checking in on us, friends meeting us at the doctor's office, a steady supply of patient listeners, well-timed distractions, invites for fun stuff, treatment strategy partners, encouragement galore, helpful research, laughter. Our people absorbed all our fears so we were free to absorb Mom's and Dad's. Our rings served us so well.

God was and still is so ever present, so ever near, so ever good. And we are taking our turn as outer rings for other folks right now, because that is how the community thing works. When someone staffs the outer rings of others, she need not worry when her day in the bulls-eye comes. She'll be surrounded by good people who love her and know the rules:

All the fear and worry can go out, and only strength and goodness can come in.

If you are in crisis with your people, you have all my love and solidarity. Set up your rings, explain the out-but-not-in Crazy Policy, and remember that God loves you and is for you.

PRAYER FOR THIS WEEK . . .

Dear God, help me be a good "ringer" for others when the time comes to do my part to help all the fear and worry go out, so only strength and goodness can come in. And thank you for my rings. Whether I'm in crisis or not, it's such a comfort that I don't have to go through life alone.

WHAT WOULD YOU DO IF YOU WEREN'T AFRAID?

Sheryl Sandberg

··

Be strong and courageous! Do not be afraid or discouraged.
For the LORD your God is with you wherever you go.

JOSHUA 1:9

Fear is at the root of so many of the barriers that women face. Fear of not being liked. Fear of making the wrong choice. Fear of drawing negative attention. Fear of over-reaching. Fear of being judged. Fear of failure. And the holy trinity of fear: the fear of being a bad mother/wife/daughter.

Without fear, women can pursue professional success and personal fulfillment—and freely choose one, or the other, or both. At Facebook we work hard to create a culture where people are encouraged to take risks. We have posters all around the office that reinforce this attitude. In bright red letters, one declares, "Fortune favors the bold." Another insists, "Proceed and be bold." My favorite reads, "What would you do if you weren't afraid?"

In 2011, Debora Spar, president of Barnard College, an all-women's liberal arts school in New York City, invited me to deliver its commencement address. This speech was the first time I openly discussed the leadership ambition gap. Standing at the podium, I felt nervous. I told the members of the graduation class that they should be ambitious not just in pursuing their dreams but in aspiring to become leaders in their fields. I knew this message could be misinterpreted as my judging women for not making the same choices I have. Nothing could be further from the truth. I believe that choice means choice for all of us. But I also believe that we need to do more to encourage women to reach for leadership roles. If we can't tell women to aim high at a college graduation, when can we?

As I addressed the enthusiastic women, I found myself fighting back tears. I made it through the speech and concluded with this:

> You are the promise for a more equal world. So my hope for everyone here is that after you walk across this stage, after you get your diploma, after you go out tonight and celebrate hard—you then will lean way in to your career. You will find something you love doing and you will do it with gusto. Find the right career for you and go all the way to the top.

As you walk off this stage today, you start your adult life. Start out by aiming high. Try—and try hard.

Like everyone here, I have great hopes for the members of this graduating class. I hope you find true meaning, contentment, and passion in your life. I hope you navigate the difficult times and come out with greater strength and resolve. I hope you find whatever balance you seek with your eyes wide open. And I hope that you—yes, you—have the ambition to lean in to your career and run the world. Because the world needs you to change it.

Women all around the world are counting on you. So please ask yourself: What would I do if I weren't afraid? And then go do it.

As the graduates were called to the stage to collect their diplomas, I shook every hand. Many stopped to give me a hug. . . .

I know my speech was meant to motivate them, but they actually motivated me. In the months that followed, I started thinking that I should speak up more often and more publicly about these issues. I should urge more women to believe in themselves and aspire to lead. I should urge more men to become part of the solution by supporting women in the workforce and at home. And I should not just speak in front of friendly crowds at Barnard. I should seek out larger, possibly less sympathetic audiences. I should take my own advice and be ambitious.

THOUGHT FOR THIS WEEK . . .

What would you do if you weren't afraid? Reread the Bible verse at the beginning of this chapter. How does reading that God is not the one behind your fear make you feel? Think about that this week and, as you do, remember the rest of the verse that says God gives "power, love, and self-discipline."

WHEN SURVIVAL ISN'T ENOUGH: A BETTER WAY TO LIVE (AND DIE)

Leslie Leyland Fields

....

There are two things a person should never be angry at;
what they can help, and what they cannot.

PLATO

How has your week gone? It's been a busy week here at fish camp. The salmonberries have come ripe, meaning forays into my island jungles and brambles, kayak trips to gather berries and fireweed, and pots of simmering jam. The eaglets are almost out of their nest entirely. The field has been cut.

And there's been excitement, too. A few days ago, it was blowing 25 mph southeast. Duncan and I were both traveling back from Larsen Bay, with wind and grey water whipping around us, the skiff pounding through every wave, our bodies rattled and wet on every landing. And then, in a moment, we were out of gas. Dead in the way-too-alive water. We had more than a mile to go. The insistent wind and waves wanted to push us to a crashing cliff-lined shore. Out came the oars, ancient oars with half the paddle gone. We looped some line around the oars for makeshift oarlocks, and both of us began coordinating our oars to keep us off the cliffs and straight down the channel. If the wind had been blowing any other direction, we would have been lost for hours, or worse.

And—a few days later, another emergency on the water. Another prayer, another crisis to survive.

And last night. Last night I trotted up the gravel hill and through the entryway to our house, and suddenly I couldn't breathe. A noxious gas nearly closed my throat. My eyes stung. I could hear a hissing sound. I stood for a few seconds, as long as I dared, looking for the source of the sound, then burst out through the front door and closed it, sucking in clean air. Ammonia. My thirty-year-old refrigerator was leaking ammonia. At high enough levels, it kills people. If it had happened in the night, while we were sleeping . . . (Imagine *that* on your tombstone: "Killed by her refrigerator"?)

We all have these moments—the rattling plane, the sinking boat, the tornado too close, the thief with the gun, the car over the edge . . . But we make it. We survive. We'll do anything to survive, anything to see another day.

Of course. We cannot give up on this life. But living is not enough. Self-preservation is not enough. It's really not.

I've had struggles of another kind this week. In between the writing, the salmon-filleting and jam-making, the feeding of a full table, the loving of children, the mending of nets, the gathering of fish, the emergencies . . . I've been visited by

Anger. Do you know what its face looks like when it bursts into the room of your heart? Have you looked it straight in the face and seen how much it looks like you?

This Anger tells me it wants to save me. It says it's for my own good. That I need it to set things right. This Anger tells me I am right—I have been wronged. It says it loves me, that I need it to survive. And I know, I have seen, how anger keeps some people alive.

I am the same as everyone else—I have cause to answer the doorbell and welcome her into my house, to give her my feather bed and pour her tea in china cups every morning, taking notes while she tells me, smiling between sips, what I've been doing wrong, how I've let injustices pass, the ways I've been robbed of my power and my rights.

There *is* a righteous anger that brings life out of death, that calls out abuse and oppression. *This* anger promises survival and happiness, but when I lean in to listen closer, I hear a hissing, like the ammonia from the fridge. My eyes sting, my throat closes, and I should run, but I don't. I stay. I think these noxious words will make me strong.

Have you seen your own face in the morning after you have slept with ammonia in the air? This Anger only wants to suffocate and kill.

I'm kicking it out of my house. I'm letting go of my fists, my rights, my wrongs. I know these words are true:

God's righteousness doesn't grow from human anger.
So throw all spoiled virtue and cancerous evil in the

garbage. In simple humility, let our gardener, God, landscape you with the Word, making a salvation-garden of your life. (James 1:19-21, MSG)

Already I can breathe. I have taken back my bed, my house, my teacups. I see this salvation-garden just outside my house this very night.

Will you join me?

Let Anger go. Kick it out. Let God make a salvation-garden of your life.

PRAYER FOR THIS WEEK . . .

Lord, help me to kick my anger to the curb. I want to stop breathing its poisonous fumes and take back my life. Plant your peace in me so that my life can grow into a beautiful garden that will refresh and nourish others.

PEDAL

Unknown

Suddenly you are doing the impossible.

ST. FRANCIS OF ASSISI

At first, I saw God as my observer, my judge, keeping track of the things I did wrong, so as to know whether I merited heaven or hell when I die. He was out there sort of like a president. I recognized His picture when I saw it, but I didn't really know Him.

But later on when I met Jesus, it seemed as though life were rather like a bike ride, but it was a tandem bike, and I noticed that Jesus was in the back helping me pedal.

I don't know just when it was that He suggested we change places, but life has not been the same since. When I had control, I knew the way. It was rather boring, but predictable. It was the shortest distance between two points.

But when He took the lead, He knew delightful long cuts, up mountains, and through rocky places at breakneck speeds; it was all I could do to hang on! Even though it looked like madness, He said, "Pedal!"

I was worried and was anxious and asked, "Where are you taking me?" He laughed and didn't answer, and I started to learn to trust. I forgot my boring life and entered into the adventure. And when I'd say, "I'm scared," He'd lean back and touch my hand.

He took me to people with gifts that I needed, gifts of healing, acceptance, and joy. They gave me their gifts to take on my journey, my Lord's and mine. And we were off again. He said, "Give the gifts away; they're extra baggage, too much weight." So I did, to the people we met, and I found that in giving I received, and still our burden was light.

I did not trust Him, at first, in control of my life. I thought He'd wreck it, but He knows bike secrets, knows how to make it bend to take sharp corners, knows how to jump to clear high rocks, knows how to fly to shorten scary passages. And I am learning to shut up and pedal in the strangest places, and I'm beginning to enjoy the view and the cool breeze on my face with my delightful constant companion, Jesus.

And when I'm sure I just can't do anymore, He just smiles and says . . .

"Pedal."

PRAYER FOR THIS WEEK . . .

God, sometimes you scare me. You often go faster than I want to go, and you take me places I'm not sure I'm ready to be . . . and I'm not in control anymore. (Truthfully, I wonder if I ever really was.) Help me to trust you, to keep pedaling, and to enjoy the adventure of journeying through life with you.

ALL THINGS NEW
Lorilee Craker

And He who sits on the throne said,
"Behold, I am making all things new."
REVELATION 21:5 NASB

In 1967, a handsome coach and a pretty young college student had a fleeting romance, or as my birth father would describe it to me forty-five years later, "four or five encounters." At some point in those encounters, I was conceived. My first parents did not love each other. In fact, they would grow to loathe each other.

Vulnerable and alone in the big city of Winnipeg, my birth mother would resolve to give birth to me in total secret; her short-term boyfriend had already fled the scene with dizzying speed.

I was born on a snowy Wednesday in March 1968 to a twenty-two-year-old mother who wept as I was taken out of her arms. She was all alone in the cab that drove her from the hospital to her shabby apartment with its mattress on the floor and a sleeping bag for a bedspread.

My story began in this mess, in the debris of lust, loathing, abandonment, and grief. Yet this messy beginning would not have the last word. I did not belong in the mess, then or now.

An Adopting Father stood tall in the rubble of my story. He had planted the seeds of redemption before my birth, before time began, and He rolled up his sleeves and got to work, making all things new.

When I was two weeks old, my parents got a call saying they could come pick me up. Actually, they were told they could come pick me out from a nursery full of newborns up for adoption, but my dad insisted the social worker pick me out himself, and that would be God's choice for their daughter.

(I recently found out that I came with a receipt. Eight dollars!)

I was brought home to belong in a humble 1964 bungalow in the super Mennonite part of Winnipeg. That's right, we were *super* Mennonites, which meant my parents spoke German (high and low), listened to dirge-y German hymns on the radio, and did not disco dance, not even once. We ate Mennonite meat buns, borscht, and zwieback, and my dad told me and my younger brother, Dan, (he cost fifteen dollars) about my dad's upbringing in Europe during World War II.

My dad was born in Ukraine during Stalin's Great Purge. The family fled when my dad was six to their ethnic Germany.

Of course, fleeing to Hitler for refuge from Stalin was like going from the frying pan to the fire. When my dad was ten, he, his parents, and his older sisters crossed the Atlantic Ocean for Halifax, Nova Scotia. He was supposed to be in grade 5 but was placed in grade 1 because he did not know English. At first, kids threw rocks at him and called him a Nazi, but he would come to belong to his new country.

He grew up to become a bookseller, with a deep passion for story and truth. The greatest thing in the world for him was to place the right story—whether it was in a novel or a nonfiction book—in the right hands at the right time. The refugee found refuge in stories. The immigrant settled in with a colony of people—his customers—who loved and revered story like he did. He belonged to his bookstore, and to the God who gave him his vocation.

My dad's story became my story; because he and my mom adopted me, I would go on to adopt a baby girl from Korea. Because an immigrant and refugee adopted me, I have a deep concern for refugees and immigrants. I know what it is, via my dad, to be welcomed as a stranger in a new land, to feel like you don't quite belong at first.

Because a bookseller and lover of story adopted me, part of my work on this earth is to write and tell stories.

Because an adoptive Father adopted us all, I know I am loved. I know He plucked me from my messy beginnings and gave me a place to belong. Thirty-six years later, he did the same thing for my girl.

Behold, He is making all things new!

PRAYER FOR THIS WEEK . . .

Dear Lord, thank you for your heart of adoption, and for making us your own, surpassingly loved. Thank you that you make us belong to each other, and to you.

GRACE IN GRIEF
Lauren Dungy

God is our merciful Father and the source of all comfort.
He comforts us in all our troubles so that we can comfort others.

2 CORINTHIANS 1:3-4

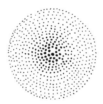

It's so hard to know what to say or do when someone is grieving over the loss of a loved one. We are often concerned about intruding or maybe saying something that doesn't help or, even worse, is insensitive and upsets them.

For some reason, it doesn't seem any easier when the grieving person is a loved one. Even then, there are simply no magic words to take the pain of the loss away, which often leaves us feeling helpless. That is true even with two spouses who know and dearly love each other. But when we don't know what to say or do, Tony and I have learned the importance of making sure we're present for each other, even if we don't say a word.

The death of his mom and dad were deep personal losses

for Tony. His parents molded and fashioned who he is, and I love how they helped nurture and grow him into the man he is today. He needed time to grieve their loss. It was the same for me when my dad passed away. Tony was so supportive, through listening to me and talking when I wanted, but he also gave me space when I needed it.

But the grief we experienced when we lost our son Jamie is beyond anything we could ever have imagined. Although we didn't understand why he took his life, we realized that God saw the whole picture, and we trusted Him to help us through this time of despair. Tony and I have spoken publicly about our Christian faith, praising God for all the good things in our life. Now that we were grieving, we realized we had an opportunity to stand up and say that, even though everything was far from great or perfect, we still trusted and loved the Lord. We knew that just as He had been with us in all the good and sad times in the past, He would be there for us in that most difficult time.

Our grieving was not by the clock. Tony and I had different moments of deep sorrow. At times, one of us seemed to do better on a particular day, only to be overcome by feelings of sadness the next day. We quickly learned to respect and support each other even when our feelings were far apart.

On those tough days, we could relate to C. S. Lewis's experience after the death of his wife, Joy:

In grief nothing "stays put." One keeps on emerging from a phase, but it always recurs. Round and round. Everything repeats. Am I going in circles, or dare I hope I am on a spiral?

But if I'm on a spiral, am I going up or down it?

How often—will it be for always?—how often will the vast emptiness astonish me like a complete novelty and make me say, "I never realized my loss till this moment"?[4]

And, of course, in the moments of greatest despair, we clung most tightly to God's promises of comfort, such as the example in 2 Corinthians above. In the end, we realized that this was the only answer we had when we wondered how we would make it through a particular day—and, in the end, we realized it was enough to carry us through.

THOUGHT FOR THIS WEEK . . .

Do you know a person or family who is grieving? How can you be present for them in their time of sorrow?

VALENTINES

Nichole Nordeman

And the greatest of these is love.

1 CORINTHIANS 13:13

This past Valentine's Day I read about an organization in New York City that was collecting homemade valentines to hand out with all the meals that would be delivered to the eighteen thousand homebound individuals in that city. Think about that. Eighteen thousand people in one city who, because of illness or age or disability, can't leave their homes. Medicine has to be delivered. Volunteers bring them every meal. If they're lucky, a family member or friend or pastor checks on them once in a while. And the best they can do is wait.

It made me so, so sad to think about those people. Sad enough to start rummaging through our glue sticks and construction paper and unleash my children to get busy making valentines to send to the Big Apple. Then it struck me that there must be homebound people right here in Tulsa. I made a quick call to Meals on Wheels and discovered that in fact about twelve hundred people every day depend on this service from inside their four walls. I realized these folks could be in my own neighborhood and I would never even know it. The lady at the agency told me that many of these elderly people do not have any visiting grandchildren and would treasure a valentine they could tape to the fridge. It would probably stay there all year long, she said.

My vision expanded.

My first idea was to collect some valentine-y art supplies—paper, stickers, ribbon, doilies—and distribute them to my son's third-grade classmates and get a few more valentines made that way. Then, like the Grinch, my project idea grew three sizes that day.

Now I wanted all the third graders in the whole school to participate. It's worth noting that at this particular school, *all the third graders* includes about three hundred kids. The size of this school is bigger than many small colleges. For the first six months, I felt like I was dropping off my baby at LAX. "Go get 'em, tiger!" I would say. Then, watching him disappear into a sea of backpacks, I would try not to throw up. It's been a tough adjustment (for me, mostly). But for my little valentines project, the numbers were in my favor.

I made a mad dash to an art supply store and got the goods. The classrooms already had markers and glue and scissors, of course. I was up until 2:00 a.m. compiling twelve big packets of valentines supplies, one for each third-grade class. (A suggestion: never try to separate a stack of three hundred wafer-thin doilies, or you will grind your molars into a nice, fine powder.)

I am trying to act quickly on crazy ideas these days. I'm finding they are often the best ones. Lord knows I have a stockpile of safe and reasonable ideas to last until Y3K. I'm tired of doling out love in level tablespoons.

Even at two in the morning, I was super-energized as I prepped and packaged the crafts. I wrote a short letter for each teacher to read to the kids about what we were doing and why. And then I left them to cut and paste as much love as they could muster.

A few days later, I picked up all the valentines (bags and bags of them) and was planning to drive them over to Meals on Wheels. Being a little ahead of schedule, I sat in my car and made the grave mistake of starting to read a few until they were soaked and soggy with my tears.

"Dear Valentine. Do you feel okay? I hope you have enough food. Maybe this will give you enough love."

"Be mine, Valentine! (Come on! You *know* you want to.)"

"If you're reading this, then you should know that you are loved, and I hope you'll be my Valentine this year."

And then, the one that sent me over the edge: "Valentine, are you sad? Would this help?"

Below the words was a teeny metal fake-ruby ring taped securely inside a purple crayon heart.

"Yours truly and forever, Timothy."

I closed my eyes and imagined someone else's grandma turning the calendar page to February 14 and swallowing a little more sadness, remembering an old sweetheart. Or a dance. Or a box of chocolates. Kept company only by her memories now, she pushes down self-pity and shakes off the invisible residue of loneliness that keeps trying to settle on her. She's hungry now. Lunch should be here soon. And so, just like every other Tuesday, she waits. And waits.

Unaware that Timothy's proposal and ring are en route.

Unaware that somewhere on the other side of Tulsa she is loved a little bit by a third grader and a forty-year-old stay-at-home mom, and the great big God of galaxies who knew her name.

Today, lunch might be worth the wait.

PRAYER FOR THIS WEEK . . .

Dear God, help me see the invisible, remember the forgotten, and reach out to those who need to know they are loved.

TWENTY-SIX ACTIVITIES OF GREAT SUBSTANCE THAT I ENJOYED IN HIGH SCHOOL

Sophie Hudson

Don't let anyone think less of you because you are young.

1 TIMOTHY 4:12

1. Rolling my hair with Conair Hot Sticks because VOLUME.

2. Watching *Moonlighting*.

3. Reading anything I could find about *Moonlighting*.

4. Putting way too much emphasis on *Moonlighting*.

5. Trying to create some serious boy drama in my life despite the fact that I didn't actually, you know, *date* anyone.

6. Offering to say the prayer at Methodist Youth Fellowship on Sunday nights so nobody would forget that I was a good little church girl.

7. Wondering what all the Jesus stuff meant outside of being a good little church girl.

8. Riding around singing along with Amy Grant's *The Collection* with my friends Elizabeth and Marion.

9. Believing with everything in me that no matter what problems I faced, AMY GRANT UNDERSTOOD THEM.

10. Choreographing ballet routines to the sound track from *St. Elmo's Fire* in order to artistically convey all my Very Deep Emotions.

11. Stopping at the Jitney Jr. on the way home from school to buy a bag of O'Grady's Au Gratin potato chips and a Mello Yello.

12. Trying to figure out why I couldn't seem to get rid of an extra twenty pounds and never really making the whole O'Grady's Au Gratin/Mello Yello connection.

13. Nodding my head a lot in sophomore year Honors Algebra II so nobody would pick up on the fact that I had no idea what was going on.

14. Going back to a regular math class my junior year because all that nodding didn't really help me pass any tests.

15. Writing excruciatingly heartfelt journal entries in which I told myself all my problems.

16. Watching *SNL* over and over with my friend Ricky and laughing until I wheezed.

17. Considering the possibility that Phil Collins really *could* see the deepest parts of my heart.

18. Singing along to the Violent Femmes cassette with my friend Amanda and feeling super-alternative in my Esprit sweater, Guess? jeans, and Tretorn tennis shoes.

19. Reading epic, hilarious notes from my friend Joni— and working *really* hard to respond with a note that would make her laugh just as much.

20. Screaming "Clang, clang, clang went the trolley"— and all the other lines from Sweeney Sisters' medleys—with Elizabeth.

21. Putting on a pair of high-waisted jeans, looking in a mirror, and marveling at how flattering they were.

22. Living in a state of delusion about that whole "flattering high-waisted jeans" thing.

23. Writing superlong letters to my out-of-town buddies Meg and Mary Helen. (Dear kids of the twenty-first century, I realize that this concept of "writing letters" might be unfamiliar to you, but it was what we had to do to communicate with people who didn't live in our town because there was no such thing as texting,

and calling someone long-distance wasn't terribly affordable for the teenage set.)

24. Staring at pretty much any passage from the Old Testament and thinking, *Well, what's that got to do with anything?*

25. Perfecting my use of royal-blue mascara.

26. Clinging to the hope I saw in Ephesians 3:20-21— but secretly doubting if it really applied to me.

Yeah, I know that last one is kinda serious.

But I went to college with some real-live questions, y'all.

And part of me kept hoping that Amy Grant would show up to answer them.

TO DO THIS WEEK . . .

Think about the activities you enjoyed in high school. Do you still do any of those things? Are you still in touch with any of your school friends? Send them an e-mail, Facebook message— even an actual card—with a "remember when" message about something you enjoyed together.

THE DISCIPLINE OF MEDITATION
Emilie Griffin

....

Oh, the joys of those who do not
follow the advice of the wicked,
or stand around with sinners,
or join in with mockers.
But they delight in the law of the LORD,
meditating on it day and night.

PSALM 1:1-2

Meditation is a form of disciplined attentiveness to God. By this concentrated spiritual activity we open ourselves to the nature of God and to his cleansing grace. Meditation is also a work of the graced imagination. Understand first that imagination is one of God's great gifts to us and has a vital place in the spiritual life. Meditation allows us to put godly imagination into play in such a way that our faith feels more alive. Often this practice allows Scripture to work in us more effectively.

One might choose for meditation some simple story of healing during the ministry of Jesus. Consider a story as brief and pointed as the healing of the man with the withered hand in Mark 3:1-5. When Jesus entered the synagogue he encountered this man. Might you put yourself in the position of this afflicted fellow? Maybe you can become one of the bystanders, waiting to see what Jesus will do. Remember how they watched him so they could criticize? So they could point out how unlawful it was to heal a man on the Sabbath? Couldn't Jesus come back the next day, they seemed to be asking, or the day after that? Possibly, in meditating on the story, you might identify with Jesus himself, hoping to take on his "with my Father all things are possible" frame of mind. Identifying in meditation with Jesus, you might say to the wretched man, "Come forward." Think how long and how habitually this man had been skulking, trying to hide his miserable hand from the rest of the community. But Jesus wants this unfortunate fellow and his withered hand out in the open where they can be seen and made whole.

Now, whatever role you are playing in the situation—whether you are the man, whether you are a bystander, whether you are identifying with Jesus himself—listen to the penetrating question: "Is it lawful to do good or to do harm on the Sabbath, to save life or to kill?" Jesus is asking us, as he always does, to consider what kind of God we are dealing with. Is this a God who wants good for us, who desires our healing and transformation? Just by throwing the bright light of the obvious onto the man with the withered hand, Jesus calls us, the bystanders, the doubters, the accepters of the status quo, onto a higher plane of faith. Had we forgotten what God is like? Had we forgotten how to trust?

"But they were silent," the Scripture says. That silence is the rebellion of people who know the answer but refuse to give it. "Jesus looked around at them with anger; he was grieved at their hardness of heart and said to the man, 'Stretch out your hand.' He stretched it out, and his hand was restored." We aren't entirely surprised by the outcome. We knew that Jesus would heal in defiance of the legitimate authorities, despite the wisdom of the age. Through meditation in silence with the power of the graced imagination, a childlike freshness comes. We grasp God's goodness in our lives.

Now meditate on the compassion of Jesus, becoming the man with the withered hand or one of the doubting bystanders. No matter which role you are drawn into, the benefits and blessings of Scripture will come home to you and lead you deeper into the abundant life.

This style of meditation has been a favorite with prayerful people over the centuries. The praying person gains the benefits, the wisdom of the story, no matter which one of the Gospel characters he or she decides to portray.

TO DO THIS WEEK . . .

Choose a story from the Bible and meditate on it as Emilie illustrates above. You might take the perspective of a different person in the story each day. At the end of the week, look back and see how you understand the story now as opposed to when you began. Is it different? The same? What have you learned from your meditation experience?

WORTHY OR WORTHLESS

Mary Southerland

....

Even before he made the world,
God loved us and chose us.

EPHESIANS 1:4

I can still remember the terror I felt each time my elementary teacher announced, "Today we will play softball at recess." My stomach clenched in dread as I contemplated the tortuous hour stretching out before me.

I hated playing softball because I was a terrible athlete! Overweight, I huffed and puffed around the bases . . . if I ever got lucky enough to hit the elusive softball. I had no idea how to wear a softball glove, so the thought of actually trying to catch the ball was terrifying. I was always assigned to the outfield, where few balls came and where I had the least chance of doing any damage.

The most horrible part of the whole experience was the

dreaded team selection process. It was always the same. First, two captains were chosen, usually Sarah and Tim because they were slender, attractive, and popular—everything I was not. Sarah and Tim would step to the pitcher's mound and begin the process of choosing their teams. I can still remember trying to look as if I didn't care that everyone around me was defecting to the other side while I waited, praying that I would hear my name called by somebody . . . anybody. I was usually one of three or four children left standing, staring at the preferred ones already taking their positions on the field. Sarah usually took pity on me and picked me before Jeff and Alicia. At least I wasn't the last one chosen.

We tend to find our identity and worth in the fact that we are chosen by someone. Over the years, I have spent a lot of life energy and costly time in an ongoing attempt to validate my identity. Much of the pain, frustration, and stress I experienced could have been avoided by simply remembering whose I am—a chosen child, a daughter of the King, and an indispensable part of God's heart. That's right! I am indispensable to no one but God. No one can take my place in my Father's heart.

The knowledge that I am chosen frees me to serve Him wholeheartedly and boldly without bowing to the unrealistic expectations imposed by others. The knowledge that He created me allows me to embrace the gifts He has given me and encourages me to strain every choice, every decision through the filter of God's perfect plan for my life. Knowing whose I am draws my attention away from both the critics and the cheerleaders in life, and fixes my gaze on the *only* one I have to please . . . God.

We come to Jesus alone. There are no "group rates" when it comes to knowing God. It's always one-on-one and very personal. What you believe about Him in the silence and stillness of your own heart is what makes the difference in your life journey. The heart is where all spiritual transactions are made and the transformation process begins.

Just think of it! God Himself supervised our formation. We were created in love—for love—with a specific and holy purpose in mind. We can rejoice with the psalmist who wrote, "Know that the LORD is God. He made us, and we belong to him; we are his people, the sheep he tends" (Psalm 100:3, NCV).

Knowing *whose* we are settles our souls and directs our steps toward the path God intended when He shaped us. You and I were created as living, fleshed-out depictions of God's love.

PRAYER FOR THIS WEEK . . .

Father, I want to know you and find your plan for my life. I choose to see myself through your eyes of love, forgiveness, and grace. I want to be the woman you created me to be. Thank you for loving me. Help me to walk each day in the knowledge that I am your child.

THE BENCH DWELLERS
Emily P. Freeman

K.I.S.S.—Keep It Simple, Sister.

UNKNOWN

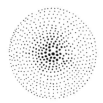

Our house sits at the top of a cul-de-sac, nestled between one neighbor who has lived here for over forty-five years and a retired couple who have been here only a few years longer than we have. On the other side of that couple are [my husband] John's brother, Frank, his wife, Mercedes, and their two young girls. They moved here first, and a few years later when this house had sat empty for a while, they suggested we try to buy it. After some stuff and things and negotiating, we did.

Our kids and our nieces were still riding tricycles at the time, so we often sat outside in the grassy center of the cul-de-sac to watch. Other kids from down the street would often come to join in, and John, Frank, Mercedes, and I pulled out lawn chairs from the garage or spread out blankets on the grass to watch the kids play.

One afternoon while John's mom was visiting, she mentioned how nice it would be to have a couple of benches in the center of the circle, more permanent seating so we wouldn't always have to drag our lawn chairs out every time the kids wanted to play. Not one to suggest ideas without taking responsibility, she showed up several days later with a bench in a box in the back of her car. Days later, a neighbor bought a matching one.

Now we have two benches facing each other in front of our houses, like our little community of seven homes finally has a living room.

As I was preparing dinner one afternoon, I glanced out my kitchen window and noticed three of our neighbors leave their homes at the same time, making their way at various shuffling speeds to meet at the benches in the middle.

I'd seen them outside in the past, chatting over newly fetched mail or exchanging comments about the weather. We enjoyed the breeze and waved at the occasional passing car. We lingered.

With dinner still cooking inside, I made my way back to the kitchen but kept my eye on them through my window. They stayed out for nearly an hour. I'd not seen them do that before. It wasn't that they didn't want to be together, but before it wasn't so easy. Now they had benches to sit on. And the benches made all the difference.

The benches didn't give them something to talk about. The benches weren't fancy, expensive, impressive, or flashy. They weren't a complicated solution to an unsolvable problem, and they didn't offer answers to difficult questions. The benches simply gave us neighbors a place to be, a place to rest, a place to come together on an ordinary day.

I've thought of this often in many areas of life when I try to make things too complicated. When I feel myself getting carried away, when I feel tempted to turn and build a city rather than accept my right-now home, I ask this simple question: *Where is the bench in this moment?*

In my work, when I see all the reasons why what they're doing over there is more important, impactful, and effective than what I'm doing over here, I'm tempted to make the platform wider and put brighter lights in the bulbs because I have to dazzle, you know. I am determined to make my work the best, the most excellent. When I want to climb the ladder, what if instead I tore the ladder apart and used the wood to build a bench?

In my relationships, when I see a need I think needs fixing, a conversation I don't know how to tackle, a grief I have no words for, I'm tempted to make things complicated and fast-moving—let's pull out the city plans, build the roadways and sidewalks straight to your heart. But people don't need fancy and flashy, they probably just want regular. They don't need a fixer, they need a journeyer. They just need to sit on a bench with someone else so they know they're not alone. I know this because it's what I need too.

TO DO THIS WEEK . . .

Does something or someone in your life need a bench? As you go through the next few days, see what needs you can identify . . . and think about whether they might have a simple solution. If you can provide a "bench," do so.

MADE NEW
Sharon Irving

I am leaving you with a gift—peace of mind and heart.
And the peace I give is a gift the world cannot give.
So don't be troubled or afraid.

JOHN 14:27

Indeed, you have called my essence forth,
    complacency no more.

And as you pour out your fragrant oil I offer my filthy
      rags of righteousness,
    placing them on the floor.

Before you, I am renewed
    in boiling darkness
    and frozen rain.

When I'm wired,
    rattled,

pressured;
squeezed in on both sides,
ripped at the seams . . .
Your hands,
    unafraid,
    reach down to the sludge of my humanity.

The promise of your presence peels from Heaven,

. . . And I am made new.

TO DO THIS WEEK . . .

Close your eyes. Take a deep breath. And another. As images seep into your mind of those places and spaces where you feel squeezed, pulled apart, or frantic, ask God to reach down into your situation—whatever you're going through—and fill you with the peace of his presence.

GOING SMALL

Allison Allen

From small beginnings come great things.
AMERICAN PROVERB

Maybe you've heard the news. I heard it on the radio several months back.

Walmart is shrinking.

It seems that some of its superstores are beginning to fall out of favor, so to counteract the loss, the retail behemoth is trying tinier-sized shops on for size, hoping to attract city dwellers and urbanites. Walmart is trying to grow bigger by literally growing smaller.

It's a mighty lesson: the power of small. And it's one that I've had the opportunity to learn a time or two.

Throughout my life, from about adolescence on, I have struggled with the gift of insomnia. Sometimes the bouts last about a week or so; other times they go on much longer.

Suffice it to say, however long the seasons of sleeplessness last, they are never welcome, and I would do just about anything to alleviate them. Several years back, I had a sleep struggle that lasted longer than most—almost three years—and as much as I hated resigning myself to a life of nighttime wakefulness, I had done so.

At some point in this marathon of insomnia, I bid on and won a gift certificate to one of those places where they run all manner of medical diagnostics on you.

You name it, they tested it: cholesterol, vision, BMI, the list went on and on. After I had been duly run through the ringer and looked like a junior higher after a particularly rough game of dodgeball, I was ushered into the doctor's office for a consultation. "Allison, the major tests will come back within ten days. So far your stress test looks good." *(Really?!)*

The doc continued, "Everything else looks to be in the normal range. Are there any health issues that you want to talk about?"

I remember telling her about the insomnia, and she actually offered up a possibility: "I think you may be vitamin D deficient."

Come on. Vitamin D? Is that the best you've got? Lady Doctor, I'm about to make a blind date with the sleep clinic, and you're talking vitamins and minerals. I need a big gun to turn this thing around.

"Really?" was the best I could muster.

She went on to explain that she had been seeing near-epidemic levels of vitamin D deficiency and that one of the nasty side effects of said lack is insomnia and its ugly twin, fatigue. She further offered that it can only be detected through a specialized blood test. I relented and gave her more blood.

Whaddaya know? A week later, the official lab letter arrived, showing my vitamin D levels to be in the bottom of the cellar, not even in the range of normal. I began taking my vitamin D prescription and started sleeping shortly thereafter.

A small thing—taking a vitamin called D—had been the answer to my problem all along.

Sometimes when we're desperate for an answer to our problems, we look for big changes—seismic shifts in spirit. Total makeovers of heart and body. The whole 180-degree turnaround. The giant reset.

We are begging for a backhoe to dig us out when what we may really need is a trowel.

In God's economy, so often it is small things, small changes, and small acts of adjustment that net the largest gains.

Restored relationships can begin with the humility of calling first. Reinvigorated health might begin with a prayer walk around the block. Unexpected friendships can bloom by sitting in a different row in church. Restored faith can be gained by believing that Jesus prays for you, every minute of every day. God dreams can be achieved by taking the next step of faith, tiny though it may be.

Mustard seeds, widow's mites, cups of cold water, fishes and loaves, little children, lost coins—all small things spoken of by Jesus to illuminate the Kingdom's largest lessons. The Bible fairly shouts "start small."

Maybe Walmart, the world's largest superstore, is on to something after all.

Something small.

TO DO THIS WEEK . . .

Look around to see what small change(s) you can implement. You might be surprised what a big difference it will make!

AN INVITATION TO GROW UP INTO GRACE
Micha Boyett

....

Amazing grace! how sweet the sound.

JOHN NEWTON

Listen, I have a gift. I can make up some killer preschool songs. If you're a three-year-old who lives in my house and you say to me, "Mommy, sing a song about 'ooogly wally offos in my socks,' I may actually belt a song that goes:

There are ooogly wally offos in my socks!
Not in my docks! Not in my pants!
Not in the sun! Not in the moon!
Not in all the places where the ooogly wally offos swoon . . .

Brooksie has learned to expect good (or at least moderately acceptable) songs to come from his mother. And so he has passed the stage of letting me sing him to sleep with sweet loving hymns or lullabies or any of the old favorites. He almost always demands an entirely new song, composed in the moment. Though sometimes, if he's feeling extra generous, he lets me sing the song I wrote for him about his dad.

I love my dad, and my daddy loves me.
He loves to run and play with me . . .

The song goes through three verses of all the fun that Brooksie and his dad have together before it comes to the final verse: the sappy, sentimental one. (I'm in charge here; I need to make somebody cry. Even if it's just me.)

Someday I will be so big and tall.
I'll be strong and I'll be brave, just like Dad.
And maybe I will have a little boy too.
I will kiss and snuggle him and this is what he'll do—
He'll sing, "I love my dad and my daddy loves me."

I know. Tears. Brooksie asked for that song the other night, and just as I was about to sing, his older brother on the top bunk chimed in. "Mom, I don't want you to sing that song. It makes me sad."

"Why does it make you sad, buddy?" I asked the little face peering over the edge of the railing.

"Because I don't want to get older and be a daddy. I want to stay a kid."

Getting older is scary. Sometimes it is simply some far-flung, floating idea. And sometimes we look in the mirror and realize that (shockingly) it is happening to us this very moment, this very hour. My almost-six-year-old gets the fear of that. We can't stay babies forever, can we? We grow and learn and get stronger and braver. And over time, each day marks us and changes us and refines us.

That face peering from the top bunk does not want to grow up. It's in human nature to fear the loss of childhood. That's why we tell the stories of brave children on big adventures, why Peter Pan—the boy who never grew up but still is somehow independent—speaks to children and grown-ups alike. This is the question that's been asked on every glossy magazine cover and will always continue to be asked: How do we grow old with grace?

Maybe the question is not how to do it with grace. Maybe it's how to grow old *in grace*. On grace. Surrounded by grace. Within God's loving, restoring presence.

I didn't have a good answer for the boy who doesn't want to grow up, who holds an already-sorrow for the loss of his present life, even though he cannot yet articulate what he's afraid of losing.

The truth is we're all afraid of losing this moment, this stage of life. We're afraid of our changing faces, our changing bodies, our changing families and friendships. We will all be asked to lose people we love. We will be asked to lose parts of ourselves we love.

And how do we enclose ourselves in grace for those coming futures? How do we grow up into grace?

I'm always undone by St. Patrick's Breastplate, that gorgeous prayer from the fifth (or some argue, the eighth) century. This is my favorite stanza:

Christ be with me, Christ within me,
Christ behind me, Christ before me,
Christ beside me, Christ to win me,
Christ to comfort and restore me.
Christ beneath me, Christ above me.
Christ in quiet, Christ in danger,
Christ in hearts of all that love me,
Christ in mouth of friend and stranger.

To grow into grace is to grow into the circle of Christ that already surrounds us. Above, beneath, behind, within. In quiet, in danger, in friendship, in the faces of strangers. We belong to the Keeper of Time. We belong to the Maker of Aging.

We are invited into the daily work of growing old—inside the one outside of Time itself, the one within and around and beside us.

The invitation is not to age with grace. No, it is to age into the grace that is already offered, already here for the taking.

PRAYER FOR THIS WEEK . . .

Thank You, God, for your amazing grace. It's such a comfort to know that no matter how old I eventually become, you are already there.

THE EXTRAVAGANT INVITATION WE'VE ALL BEEN WAITING FOR

Jennifer Dukes Lee

....

"Now go out to the street corners and invite everyone you see."
So the servants brought in everyone they could find, good and
bad alike, and the banquet hall was filled with guests.

MATTHEW 22:9-10

So, I've been having this dream.

And in the dream, there's a long table stretching out under an open sky. The heavens are coated with stars, so many that we don't need to light the ivory tapers that someone twisted into those crystal holders. The table is covered in a white cloth that blows in the summer breeze, and all the people are laughing and carrying on. I carry pottery heaped high and steaming to that long rectangle in the grass. My hands smell like garlic, and the air smells like lilacs.

I'm not wearing shoes, because I want to feel the grass between my toes when I walk back and forth to the kitchen.

The little boys are burping. Some of the women are

dressed in sequined gowns, like they got all gussied up for a ball to be held in a marbled room somewhere. Sitting beside them? New friends who came wearing their dirty, threadbare T-shirts with screen-printed sayings like, "Go Wildcats" or "Life is Good." There's a Mercedes parked next to a rusty Pinto. I nearly trip over a pair of crutches propped up near the head of the table.

Everyone got invited, and almost everyone came. We had hoped and prayed they would. We had wanted them to taste the feast. And we know for sure that someone had hoped and prayed for us, too.

There was this awareness hanging in the air: It cost someone a lot to make a space for us at the table. We came with empty pockets, because the host told us that this was all a gift.

The price of admission? Our hunger.

In the dream, a bunch of us had taped a sign to a barrel and rolled it out to the middle of Main Street. "Come One and All!" The poor, the lame, the drunk, the rich, the holy. The naughty kid, the valedictorian, the blind guy, the beggar, and the CEO.

There was room for all, and all of us had been waiting our whole lives for this. We didn't know it until now.

The table seems intimate—like it could fit in the corner of some small diner—yet it stretches for miles because the host didn't pick favorites. He wants us all.

When I touch the table, it feels like it has a heartbeat.

From the grass, I watch them come round the corner, out by the wizened oaks. Some have tears in their eyes. A guy in a three-piece suit drops to his knees on the sidewalk when he sees a chair with his name on the back of it. An old woman throws back her head and starts singing a song I've never heard before but know. There's a poem hanging from the branches, and music slides down from the sky. It falls like dew on our skin.

And the fireflies dance around our heads.

I see no masks. No one pretends or tries to prove a thing. We showed up fragile and hungry. We are safe here.

"Bring your mess," says the banner flapping in the breeze. "Your mess doesn't disqualify you. It's your ticket in."

All of us, we know we are a mess, and when we get to thinking about it, we are astonished at the invitation to a table so sacred. The host lets us help serve the dinner, which floors me. And so we keep bringing out potatoes, and green beans, and filet mignon, and my hands shake a little at the honor of carrying food to the table.

There is more than enough for everyone.

In the dream, someone clears his throat, and the sound echoes down the table, a hallowed rumble. He says: "Have a seat, please." We all find a place at the table. A holy silence falls around our ears, and then down to our ankles.

Everyone is barefoot, and all the bare feet are under one long table, and that's the part that makes me cry every time.

Your mess doesn't disqualify you. It's your ticket in.

PRAYER FOR THIS WEEK . . .

Thank you, Lord, that there is a place at the table for anyone who will come. Help me remember that, really, in some way we are all a mess—but you can handle that. You love me even in my messiness. Help me extend that love to the other messy people I encounter this week.

USE YOUR WORDS
Shauna Niequist

....

*These words dropped into my childish mind as if you should
accidentally drop a ring into a deep well. I did not think of
them much at the time, but there came a day in my life when
the ring was fished up out of the well, good as new.*
HARRIET BEECHER STOWE

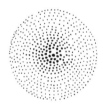

I ran into a friend I haven't seen in years. He influenced me
very deeply in all sorts of ways in one particular season of
life, and then there he was, unexpectedly, standing there in
the sunshine in Phoenix. We didn't make small talk—it was
clear that he had just a minute before he had to leave. After
he hugged me, he kept his hands on my shoulders for just a
second and said, "I'm so proud of you. I'm *so* proud of you."
I drank up the kindness of his words, so surprised by them.
I bet I could tell you every word of our short conversation.

Because he spent his words wisely. He knew that his words
would be important to me, and so in just a few minutes, he
spent them. He recalled conversations we had more than ten

years ago, about how I wanted to be a writer but could hardly even say it out loud for fear that someone like me could never do something like that.

He told me about friends of his who'd read my books and talked to him about them. And at the beginning and the end of the conversation, he looked straight at me and said these words: *I'm so proud of you.*

I think sometimes we shy away from words like this because it's awkward, or because we don't want to make things all serious. We don't say anything because we assume people don't really care that much what we think, or because we don't want to seem parental—doesn't *proud* sound a little bit like you're talking to a twelve-year-old?

Maybe it does. But the self-conscious twelve-year-old in me was absolutely thrilled to hear that someone I respected so deeply thought I was doing a good job. His words mattered to me.

Later that night, I was sitting with a friend, another writer. She was trying to make a hard decision, feeling a little bit pressured by her publisher. At one point, I said, "Listen: you're an incredible writer." I saw a look of shock on her face. "You know that, right? Don't people tell you all the time that you're a very, very special writer?"

"No one tells me that," she said. "Are you crazy? No one says that."

And I thought of my old friend, and our conversation earlier that day. His words were still ringing in my ears, making me smile every time I thought of them, like a twelve-year-old.

I'm not in any way the impressive person he is, not by a long shot, but I wondered if my words could do the same thing in her that his words did in me.

So I looked right into her eyes and said, "Listen: You're special. Your writing is important, and it changes people, and it's changed me. Your writing matters."

And I knew by her face that I didn't need to be famous in order for my words to be valuable to her. Words are valuable, and everyone needs to know that they're loved, that someone's proud of them, that someone sees the magic that makes them *them*.

So this is my challenge for you: *Use your words.* Use them today. For someone you love, someone you're proud of, someone who needs to know they matter.

Everyone needs to know they matter.

TO DO THIS WEEK . . .

Use your words. Send someone a note or just pick up the phone or knock on someone's front door. Look that person right in the eye and say, "I'm proud of you. I'm cheering for you. I'm thankful for you. You're special."

SERVING COMMUNION
Katie Savage

....

When all is said and done,
how we loved is how we'll be remembered.
JENNIFER DUKES LEE

My friend Maria has had a long history with depression, and she was dealing with it again after she experienced a sudden miscarriage. In order to help her through it, I did the only think I could think of: I brought food. Grocery bags full of the fixings for fish tacos, to be precise. I planned to spend the evening cooking for the family, helping with the house and the kids so Maria and her husband could have a bit of peace. It would be like if Paula Deen and Mother Teresa teamed up.

When I arrived at Maria's that afternoon, the atmosphere felt different. Usually, there are choo-choo trains strewn around the couch and library books stacked up on the dining room table—the house has the wonderful feeling of being perpetually in midplay. That day, although the trains and the books were still strewn about, they seemed less buoyant: laundry and dishes and stale air were more prevalent, and Maria was in the bathroom, crying. And just so you know, it is way easier to help your friends when they entertain you with their sarcastic wit and delicious margaritas than when they are inconsolable and weary. So I blame her.

When her twin boys got home from kindergarten, they were fighting—loudly and obnoxiously. And loudly. Most of the time, they get home with funny questions and surprising anecdotes about other kids in their class. This was not at all how things would go for Paula Deen, and I spent more of my energy trying to coax the boys into better moods than I did adding butter to anything. Her baby girl wouldn't stop crying. The oven was broken. When Maria's husband got home, I had to ask him to cook the fish on the grill outside. You know, as a relaxing way to end a stressful day at work and an emotionally haggard week, why don't you cook the dinner that I was going to cook for you? My plans to care for Maria and her family that night were slowly unraveling.

By the time the food was finally on the table—an hour or so later than planned—we were all exhausted. We sat around the table, staring at each other with blank looks. The boys—who, I'll have you know, are known to eat weird things like shiitake mushrooms and quinoa and tofu—wouldn't eat the fish. The baby was still crying. But still, somehow, the food helped.

The phrase *body of Christ* is used in the Bible in three major ways—Jesus uses it to describe the bread broken in Communion, Paul uses it to describe the Church and how it should function, and, of course, the phrase denotes Jesus' actual, physical body. The one he used to eat and drink with the tax collectors, to walk among Gentiles and Jews, to die on the cross. Understanding this threefold meaning is vital, I think, to understanding our calling: to "feed one another constantly from [our] own bodies, [our] own plates, [our] own inadequate stores of insufficient food." It is easy with those we love the most, and I remember this now when I take Communion—holding Genevieve, a second beautiful child, one who will receive the elements secondhand, through my own body. A miracle on many levels. It is harder to share food with a stranger, harder still with an enemy. Or people who double-dip. Or someone who insists on using the phrase *booya* without even a touch of irony. But that is what we, the Church, are meant to do.

Maria needed to be served Communion, I think. But more than that—and intrinsic in the act of "doing" Communion at all—she needed to "sit at the table," as they say. She needed fellowship and community and friends who might act as the very hands of Christ to her. We all do. In the same sense, I needed to serve her Communion, needed to remember Christ yesterday, tomorrow, and yes, today. Eating together, in this sense, is extraordinary and sacrificial and pure and good, even when the oven is broken and the kids are crying and you're all in really bad moods.

TO DO THIS WEEK . . .

Think about who you know who needs a friend. What can you do to "act as the very hands of Christ" to that person? Set aside time on your calendar to serve that person this week.

THE SLEEP THAT NOURISHES WISDOM

Patsy Clairmont

....

Silence is the sleep that nourishes wisdom.

FRANCIS BACON

When Luci Swindoll told me one of her favorite inventions was the alphabet, I knew we would always be friends. I love words. I'm a bona fide verbiage collector. I love small words like *gnu*, descriptive words like *dollop*, and filler words like *thingamajigs* and *whatchamacallits*.

There's something magical about lining up letters and finding the very thing you want to say. So imagine the jolt I got when a couple of my friends showed up at a conference sporting "On Voice Rest" badges.

"What does that mean?" I puzzled.

They rolled their eyes and pointed at the confusing script.

"On Voice Rest," I squawked. Still befuddled I asked, "But does that mean you're actually not going to talk?"

179

They nodded. I was almost silenced, but then I rallied and decided I could talk for all three of us. So I was chatting away when one of them got up, walked over to me, and pulled from her pocket a backup badge and pinned it on my collar. *Harrumph.*

C'mon, not talk? Think. About. It.

I read once about a movie actor who fasted from words on Wednesdays. He said it added such a flurry of creative energy to his work and it helped him be more word sensitive when he did speak.

Secretly, I admired his choice, but I have yet to duplicate it. I have, however, remained silent on two-hour flights, only to get off and magpie anyone within a ten-foot perimeter. It's like the accrued word count within me had percolated in my silence until when I disembarked I erupted into a volley of caffeinated chat.

I do have a propensity to go on and on. I know that. It's like I have no edit button, when in truth I know it's a matter of changing gears (slowing my pace) and installing a conscious (Holy Spirit) awareness of my need to at least minimize my word count.

Voice rest has multiple benefits.

- Those who have grown weary of our deluge are relieved.
- We listen more closely (because we are not busy crafting our response).

- Our new discipline will spill over into other frayed areas of our life.
- People's trust in us grows.
- And our center stills. We feel less frantic and, surprisingly, more heard.

So what about a wordless Wednesday or having a mute button installed for Monday mornings? Or being silent long enough to hear what God's curriculum is for us?

Think about it. I am.

TO DO THIS WEEK . . .

Can you go for a day without talking? If that's not possible, what about a morning, an afternoon, or—for you really chatty types—an hour? This week, take one day and give it a try. Take note of what you notice about how you feel, how those around you behave, and what you learn when you take a break from talking.

EMILY DICKINSON, MAY 15

Lauren F. Winner

I shall know why, when time is over,
And I have ceased to wonder why;
Christ will explain each separate anguish
In the fair schoolroom of the sky.
EMILY DICKINSON

Some of my most beloved saints are not really saints—no feast days in the church, no special prayers written on their behalf—so I improvise. I like to mark their deaths. Today is the death of the belle of Amherst.

Emily Dickinson has compelled me since I was tapped to play her in a school production at age nine. I wanted to play Betsy Ross, who had more lines, actual dialogue, and who got to sew; my entire role consisted of sitting at a desk, leaping up from said desk, and declaiming a sixteen-line ode to nature, "I'll tell you how the sun rose."

In the end, clad in my mother's white Lanz nightgown, I performed my small part with a melodramatic verve that would have made Joan Crawford seem subtle, and I felt bereft when the play was over. I decided I liked being Emily Dickinson, the recluse, because after all I was on stage alone—Betsy had to share the stage with George Washington. This experience inaugurated a thus-far lifelong troika: a) I secretly long to try out for community theater, but don't dare; b) I battle regularly, but probably not regularly enough, my love of melodramatic declamation, my tendency to perform rather than listen, my desire to be the sole object of an audience's enthralled attention; and c) I am obsessed with Emily Dickinson, with her seclusion, with her small world of desk and window, with what she could make words do, how she bent them; with her beguiling consonant rhyme and eye-rhyme, a soundscape where *more* and *despair* are coupled; *wind* and *God*.

For the anniversary of her death, a few friends and a few students come over. Dina brings ginger cake, made with the recipe Dickinson herself used, all those ginger cakes she lowered down out of her window into the waiting hands of neighborhood children: 3 cups of flour, 1 tablespoon of ginger, 1 cup of molasses, butter, cream, baking soda, salt. I read a poem about forgetfulness; Sarabeth reads a poem about a bird; Karin reads a letter Dickinson wrote, late in life, to a judge whom she might or might not have wanted to marry: "On subjects of which we know nothing, or should I say *Beings* . . . we both believe, and disbelieve a hundred times an Hour, which keeps Believing nimble."

Here over the ginger cake it seems to me that Dickinson

was describing my own state, and my own hope: the winding back and forth between belief and disbelief, the hope that such peregrinations won't drive me crazy or make me cynical but rather keep me nimble. What strikes me, too, about these words from Dickinson is that for all the hundred-times-an-hour, she doesn't seem frantic; she doesn't seem to be wringing her hands about this back-and-forth, or anxiously aspiring to a more settled belief or disbelief.

Later that night, I find myself thinking, *maybe this is a way of inhabiting faith that is, indeed, faithful; that is generative.* Maybe God has given some people belief like a pier, to stand on (and God has given those people's steadiness to the church, to me, as a reminder, as an aid), and maybe God has given others something else: maybe God has given to some this humming sense that we know nothing, this belief and disbelief a hundred times an hour, this training in nimbleness (and maybe that is a gift to the church too).

PRAYER FOR THIS WEEK . . .

Dear God, just as the father who brought his son to Jesus for healing said, "Lord, I believe; help my unbelief!" (Mark 9:24, NKJV). Despite what he considered his lack of faith, you did heal his son. Thank you for continuing to work in our lives even when we don't always feel we have enough (or strong enough or the right kind of) faith.

MASTERY?
Connally Gilliam

If you aren't in over your head,
how do you know how tall you are?
AUTHOR UNKNOWN

In addition to believing that I must—to gain a solid sense of identity—have some kind of "thing" that I can point to (think: marriage or career contribution), I have also believed that I should exhibit a fundamental mastery of this elusive "thing." I got my first master's degree at twenty-five, and I'm looking at my second at fifty. In some coach's training I've had, they've spoken about being a "master coach." When I taught public high school, we aspired to be "master teachers." And a friend of mine who plays the violin has more than once spoken of the maestro, simply an Italian word for "master." Mastery is desirable and possible, right?

The problem is, I've secretly thought I needed to master

more than this elusive thing. I've believed that I must master life itself. I'm laughing as I write this: *Seriously, am I that performance oriented?* Yep. One professor friend of mine has spoken of our culture's twisted (my word) cultivation of an "audience-based subjective sense of self." Put differently—if a whole bunch of people see me and clap, *I am.* So it's simple: Master life, people will see and clap, and then *I am.* Simple, except that it has proven impossible.

New challenges pour in daily: loving well my visiting nineteen-year-old nephew whose music choices, technology preoccupation, and affinity for movies where things blow up are not natural connects for me. Trying to get to know an online dating guy who lives three hundred miles away and may or may not call again. Waiting on my employer for a potential job redefinition. Having yet another conversation about navigating sexuality in our culture. Walking with a friend who has incurable cancer.

The list on nonmastery is endless.

But what I do have in Jesus Christ is access to *the* Master. A friend of mine often begins his prayers like this: "Dear Master . . ." Such an address can sound foreign or even threatening (I think of *12 Years a Slave*). But, if possible, setting aside possible connotations from the concept's abuse, think with me for a moment of *the* Master into whose joy we get to enter, the one who is forgiving and merciful, the one who will return for us, the only one before whom any of us falls or stands.

Can you, like me, get any sense of comfort from knowing that He is *the* Master? Any peace from encountering *this*

Maestro who in loving omniscience can lead with nephews and online men and work and sexuality and cancer? Does it bring you any courage to recognize that *He* is the "I am," and that it is in following, before mastering, that you and I begin to find some sense of solid self?

If this holds any allure, it might be worth asking yourself: *What area(s) of life have I assumed I should have mastered by now? Or what mastery might I be seeking that I have secretly believed will somehow make me more real, more solid, more safe, more valuable, more . . . ?* And then pause to consider: *What might it look like for me to invite the one with consummate, eternal mastery into my current challenges, asking Him to lead, seeking to listen, and then willingly following?*

This is not a recipe for perfect peace or instant identity. Peace and identity also elude perfect mastery. But it is a way I'm learning to walk forward, increasingly solid and secure with *the* Master who before time began has been, is, and will always be *the* I am.

TO DO THIS WEEK . . .

Make a list of things you feel you should have mastered, but haven't. Write down the things you're still hoping to master. Next, describe what you hope to gain from mastering these things. Finally, ask God for insight about which (if any) of those things you really need to pursue. Remember: Your worth does not depend on your skill set; it has already been determined by Jesus, who loved you enough to die for you.

THE CRAZY QUILT
Melody Carlson

The best antiques are old friends.

SEEN ON A SIGN

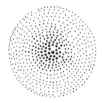

I have an old quilt made by my father's grandmother. It's not a beautiful quilt, and all the fabric appears to be quite old. But I love it.

The pieces are probably leftover scraps from Aunt Fran's apron, little Mary's Easter dress, or Grampa's favorite shirt. They are odd shapes and sizes. Some nameless shapes have hooks and curves, long slivers of fabric painstakingly sewn with dozens of meticulous stitches. A few tiny patches are smaller than my thumbnail. Some of the fabric is very plain with dull colors. I can just hear some tired mother say, "But, dear, it's a very serviceable cloth. . . ." while her daughter frowns at the new school dress. Other pieces are bright and cheery, like snippets of birthdays, summer vacations, and fun times gone by. A few fancier pieces are satiny smooth with embossing or embroidery; they seem to whisper of weddings, dances, a first kiss . . .

My father's grandmother was nearly blind, and perhaps that explains why the shades appear haphazardly arranged and almost seem to shout at each other. I wonder if she ever realized what her creations looked like, or did she simply go by touch? They do have an interesting texture—smooth next to bumpy, seersucker alongside velvet; and all over the quilt hundreds of tiny stiches, almost invisible to the eye, pucker ever so slightly.

If I were blind, I would like to make quilts like this.

Recently my own family relocated to a new town, and I was in bed with the flu, wrapped in my great-grandmother's crazy quilt. I felt sorry for myself and I missed the friends I'd left behind. Deep down, I knew it was partly my own fault—I hadn't taken steps to establish new friendships. Several acquaintances seemed willing, but I was holding back, hesitating. . . .

As I studied the crazy quilt, I thought of the many friends I'd had throughout my life. Some felt a bit scratchy and rough like a sturdy piece of wool, but in time they softened—or I became used to them. Others were delicate like silk and needed to be handled with care. Some were colorful and bright and great fun to be with. A few special others felt soft and cozy like flannel, and they knew how to make me feel better.

Many of my friends have only been around for a season.

So often I've had to leave them behind, or they leave me! And yet, in my heart, I know they are friends for life. If I met them on the street tomorrow, we would hug and laugh and talk nonstop. It would seem like yesterday.

And that's because God has sewn them into my heart.

I pulled the old quilt closer around me, comforted and warmed by my memories. Surely, my own masterpiece—this quilt of friendships I fretted over—was not nearly finished. I would make new friends in this town. And like my great-grandmother, trusting her fingers to lead her, I would, by faith, reach out.

TO DO THIS WEEK . . .

Take a few minutes to think about the various friendships you've enjoyed over the course of your life.

Picture them as different patches in your "crazy quilt" of life. How are they alike? How are they different? As each friend comes to mind, thank God for the time you shared (or are still sharing) together.

CINDERELLA: CARPE DIEM! (CARPE PUMPKIN! CARPE THAT SHOE!)

Ginger Kolbaba

As you go along your own road in life,
you will, if you aim high enough, also meet resistance. . . .
But no matter how tough the opposition may seem,
have courage still—and persevere.

MADELEINE ALBRIGHT, FORMER U.S. SECRETARY OF STATE

Little Cinder Maid had a rough life. Mom died. Dad died. An orphan, she was left to the mercy of malicious step-relations who treated her like a servant. But Cinderella didn't let her past misfortune or present circumstances get in the way of her pursuing, yes, seizing upon the could-bes.

When Fairy Godmother appeared, Cinderella didn't think twice about accepting her invitation for an extreme makeover. And by obediently following Fairy Godmother's bibbidi-bobbidi-boo orders to leave the castle ball by midnight, she guaranteed herself a position as the future Mrs. Prince Charming.

Cinderella said yes: to the dress, to the risk, and to the reward.

As our model, she now tells us, "Take hold of the moment! Don't allow fear of the unknown to get in the way of becoming who you were rightfully created to be."

Amen, I say. Risk reaching for the stars. Risk for the possibility of a stronger and brighter future. Risk for the wisdom that comes through the success and the failure. Risk for the promise that stagnation won't take over in your spirit and soul. Take a chance!

But I also know it isn't always as easy as Cinderella makes it seem. For instance, whenever I've taken a risk, I've never once met a mouse who could sew. I've never seen a pumpkin with a built-in transmission. And I've never met a singing and jolly godmother who showed up waving a wand and offering me glass stilettos. It's usually a little more complicated. And less animated.

My friend Kim took a chance when she and her husband, Jahn, decided to adopt a little boy from Ukraine. Everything seemed to go according to plan. They submitted their paperwork, paid their fees, went through the background checks and home inspection, and then flew to Ukraine to greet their family's new addition. But once in Ukraine, things started to fall apart. The adoption went through, but a corrupt prosecutor, who didn't want an American to take one of Ukraine's children, challenged the adoption orders. That meant that Kim's son, Jake, wasn't allowed to leave the country.

Rather than return home without her son, she chose to remain in Ukraine for a year—where things only continued to spiral downward. She ended up hiding from the authorities, had a warrant out for her arrest (because she refused to return Jake to the orphanage), and suffered bouts of loneliness and spiritual despair.

People kept encouraging her to leave and go home, that things would work themselves out, that she and Jahn could always adopt another child, that this was too difficult. She should just let it go.

But she was all in. She had taken a chance, and she wasn't going to back out. She knew that God was with her in this journey—even though she didn't always sense his presence or see his hand at work.

After a year, an arrest, and a dramatic escape, she made it home with her son. Today, she'll tell you it was the hardest—but the best—thing she's ever done.

"Taking that risk and committing to it—when everyone else thought I was crazy—was something I'm glad I did," Kim told me. "I learned so much about faith and about what real, gut-level joy looks like. And best of all, I have a beautiful son. By obeying God to take that chance in Ukraine, I learned the extent God will go to move mountains for one abandoned child, and how God will stop at nothing to show how much he loves and cares for orphans."

If we want to experience mind-blowing joy, then we have to be willing to take risks.

GOOD RISK/NOT-SO-GOOD RISK

GOOD RISK: Making a solid case in front of your boss of why you need a promotion/raise.

NOT-SO-GOOD-RISK: Asking for a promotion/raise after you post on Facebook that your boss passed gas in the weekly meeting.

GOOD RISK: Asking your mother-in-law to lunch to get to know her better.

NOT-SO-GOOD-RISK: Taking her to a seafood place when she's allergic to shellfish and then making her pay the bill.

GOOD RISK: Saying yes to God's nudge to do short-term missions work.

NOT-SO-GOOD-RISK: Doing the missions work by making reservations at a Bahamas Sandals resort with plans to do your devos by the pool.

GOOD RISK: Deciding you want to spice up your marriage by getting closer to your hubby.

NOT-SO-GOOD-RISK: Parading in front of the television set in the middle of March Madness.

TO DO THIS WEEK . . .

As you assess potential rewards (and the risks that come with them), know that you are not alone. You can ask God for help.

James 1:5 says, "If you need wisdom, ask our generous God, and he will give it to you."

You might say something like this: "Lord, help me clearly see the rewards and risks before me—the good ones and the not-so-good ones—and give me wisdom to know which ones I should go for and which I should let pass me by."

AIN'T NO PARTY LIKE A WRAPPING PARTY

Melanie Shankle

....

We are best friends. Always remember that if you fall,
I'll pick you up . . . just as soon as I quit laughing.

AUTHOR UNKNOWN

Every year, right around September, Gulley and I get together for a calendar meeting to plan our annual Christmas Shopping Weekend, complete with the Wrapping Par-tay. (It must be pronounced just like the women used to say it in the Walmart commercial. This is critical.) And yes, I meant to capitalize it because it is an event. For almost as long as we've been friends, we have designated one weekend in early December as an exclusive girls' weekend, when we spend forty-eight hours finishing all our Christmas shopping and then eating a variety of cheeses on Saturday night while we wrap every last present.

Back in our college days, most of this weekend was spent

looking for a cute outfit to wear on New Year's Eve and charging it to our dads' Visa cards. Shout-out to the Guess boot shoes of 1992! But as our lives changed and the bulk of our Christmas shopping became focused on our kids, we began most of these weekends at Toys"R"Us. Rumor has it that's where a kid can be a kid, and while that is all good and fine, it's also a place where mothers have been known to instantaneously double up on their birth control pills. I can't explain how loud and chaotic the store is on a Friday night two weeks before Christmas. There are kids crying and begging in every single aisle. It honestly feels less like a quality shopping experience and more like a hostage situation.

Many times, Gulley and I just end up standing next to our cart and gazing blankly at a huge wall of Star Wars toys while she asks me if I think the DC-17 Skywalker Fighter Jet (probably not its real name, because PLEASE) is better than the Rebel Fighter blah, blah, blah, and I'm all like, "Why are you speaking to me in a foreign language? No comprendo el Star Wars." This is usually about the time when we realize that we are overwhelmed not only by all the kids being kids but also by the fact that Toys"R"Us is clearly charging upwards of five dollars more per toy than Target does.

However, even in Target, things aren't necessarily easier. The prices might be better, but often we still have no clarity about whether Rebel Forces are the good guys or if a Tinkerbell Styling Head is better than an Island Princess Barbie Styling Head or how some of those little stuffed animal puppies manage to look trampy even though they're just dogs. . . .

Over the years we have looked for every hot toy you can imagine. We've come home and bid for hard-to-find things on eBay, we've walked miles at various malls and shopping centers, we've talked each other down from buying absurd toys in a frantic attempt to make Christmas magical, and we've kept track of Christmas lists that would make Santa Claus seem unorganized. We take this seriously. We are two women on a mission, and we only make occasional stops to refuel with Diet Coke and a sugar cookie. . . .

After all our shopping is completed on Saturday night, we usually finish at the grocery store to buy all kinds of unhealthy snacks and stuff to make cookie dough that will be eaten straight from the bowl and never baked into actual cookies. Then we stay up into the wee, small hours of the night wrapping presents and tying bows and losing multiple pairs of scissors and rolls of tape as we watch movies and discuss everything from the politics of elementary school to college football to my ongoing dilemma over whether I should have bangs.

I mention this tradition because I highly recommend it for every woman. It takes something that can be frustrating and time consuming and turns it into a fun girls' weekend that you can totally play up to your husband as "working hard to give the family a wonderful Christmas" because you're just that selfless. And if you're like me, you can even offer to buy a few Christmas presents for yourself while you're out. Plus, our kids get so excited to see all those beautifully wrapped presents under the Christmas tree when they get home from wherever their fathers have taken them for the weekend.

Gulley and I realized last year that we didn't really need to go to Toys"R"Us anymore. Our kids are a little bit older and all about the electronics instead of the Star Wars action figures or Barbie dolls. I think it made both of us a little sad, because those little years went by so fast and nobody wants a toy kitchen anymore. But that's the beauty of walking through life with a friend. When you realize that one stage might be ending and another one beginning, she helps you look at the bright side. And the bright side looks a lot like Christmas shopping that basically consists of buying a bunch of iTunes gift cards and having more time to see several movies in one weekend.

Of course, we'll still stay up late on Saturday night to wrap the gift cards anyway because, after all, it's a tradition.

TO DO THIS WEEK . . .

What upcoming activity do you dread? How can you turn it into a party? Brainstorm whom to invite, what snacks might be involved, and how you can change a chore into a celebration. But don't stop with thinking about it—make it happen. Who knows? You might start a new tradition of your own.

GOD'S VOICE

Jen Hatmaker

They said, "Look, the LORD our God has shown us his glory and greatness, and we have heard his voice."

DEUTERONOMY 5:24

My adopted Ethiopian daughter, Remy, loves *Jessie* on the Disney Channel, but she cannot for the love of everything good and pure figure out real versus pretend when it comes to shows and movies. Our conversation yesterday (I've endured enough of this exact discussion to qualify me for sainthood):

"Jessie is real life?"

"Ugh."

"She is fake?"

"She is a character. The girl who plays her is real."

"She is not dead?"

"No."

"But I love her! Why is she not alive?"

"She is. But Jessie is just made up. That girl is pretending."

"She killed Jessie?"

"Oh, my."

"Oh! She is a drawn cartoon?"

"No, she is human."

"In heaven?"

"Okay. Yes. Fine. Jessie is a live human in heaven."

We have a clear communication problem, partly because she is a nine-year-old interrogator, and partly because we grew up speaking different languages. Finding ways to hear and understand each other is something we work at every. single. day.

Believers often have similar problems hearing God, whether correctly, clearly, or at all. Does he still speak, and if so, is that voice for everyone? And if it is, why do only some believers seem to hear it?

If I've heard any one struggle with hearing God's voice, it's this: How do I know it's God? How do I know it's not me? Or worse yet, the enemy? Sometimes it all sounds the same, and discerning God's voice from its rivals can be daunting at best and disastrous at worst. Let's work through some strong indicators of God's voice, and learn to recognize them and notice when they're absent.

Let's first consider the *quality* of God's voice, his general manner of speaking. With humans, this marks the force of a voice: high, low, loud, soft, strong, subtle. It affects the way a voice is received. We need only to look at Jesus and how he affected people when he spoke. He never pleaded or pandered; there was never a sense of hesitancy. He moved unmovable people. Even the demons obeyed, for they *simply couldn't help it.*

We can distinguish the quality of God's voice by the weight of authority with which it hits our souls. We are immediately impressed with the certainty of what he has said. Even against our nature, we are compelled to follow, bend, release, obey. When God speaks, it rings strong, and we sense inwardly its power. Our heart and mind responds: Yes.

E. Stanley Jones said, "Perhaps the rough distinction is this: The voice of the subconscious argues with you, tries to convince you; but the inner voice of God does not argue, does not try to convince you. It just speaks, and it is self-authenticating. It has the feel of the voice of God within it."[5]

Beyond the strong quality of God's voice, it also bears a certain *spirit.* It's the spirit of a heavenly Parent who adores his children: loving, patient, jealous for our safety, protective, reasonable, so compassionate it almost hurts. We've distorted his voice and often expect disappointment—if he speaks to us at all. Please hear this: "There is now no condemnation for those who are in Christ Jesus" (Romans 8:1, NIV). If you are hearing shame and guilt, that is certainly *not* the voice of God. He is incapable of speaking to us like that.

The spirit of his voice strains toward our spiritual health, whatever that looks like in the moment. It gently mends what's broken. It directs us back from our dangerous wanderings. It builds up, heals. As Jesus modeled, it's not permissive, as he loves us too much to leave us in our sin. Yet there is no condemnation. It remains intact in the midst of discipline.

Finally, God's voice is distinguished by the content of his words. While we might not initially recognize his voice based solely on *what* he says, this much we know: God's directions will never contradict the Bible. He won't lead us in a way that harms his Kingdom or destroys others. God doesn't speak contrary to his nature.

God won't ask you to hate, lie, cheat, judge. He won't have you hurt his people. God wouldn't tell you to act in retaliation. He doesn't tempt you. And God surely won't justify those if they happened to you. Don't believe "God told me to" on any of those assaults to his character.

Over time, we develop an ear for God's voice, realizing that it is often gentle but not silent, firm but not hysterical. He need not resort to theatrics to speak to us. When we get still, quiet, small, God's words break through, leading us into the Kingdom and changing our lives.

"God's voice thunders in marvelous ways; he does great things beyond our understanding" (Job 37:5, NIV).

Thunder on, God.

We're listening.

PRAYER FOR THIS WEEK . . .

God, help me to listen for your voice this week. I'm amazed (and thrilled) that you want to talk to me. Please help me quiet myself enough to hear what you have to say. I'm listening. . . .

CHRISTMAS NUTS

Phyllis Tickle

Often, the less there is to justify a traditional custom,
the harder it is to get rid of it.

MARK TWAIN

It was the hard spring freeze that did it, everyone said. I don't know enough about pecans to gauge the accuracy of that explanation, but I do know that there were no pecans. The trees never bloomed, never tasseled, never made nuts.

There were no long evenings in the kitchen in early December, no brown fingers, no aching shoulders. Instead, we took out of the freezer the nuts we had put back in the year before. We made candies and fruitcake and baked the nut pies for Christmas dinner, and I gave the whole thing no thought beyond a vague sense of relief until three days before Christmas when twelve-year-old Sam Jr. remarked morosely, "I missed the pecans this year."

"Whatever for? We have a freezer full!"

"I missed doing them," and he walked out the door to do his evening chores in the hen house.

I looked at [my husband] Sam and he looked at me. The next afternoon he came home from town with three big sacks full of the worst-looking unshelled pecans I have ever seen. Where he managed to beg or buy them he never said and I never asked, but we all sat down—the five of us still at home—and interrupted our lives to let the nuts in.

We cracked, shelled, and sorted nuts we didn't need for dishes we wouldn't eat and sacked more for a freezer that couldn't hold them. We baked one more fudge cake and roasted nuts for the nursing stations at the hospital (which made Sam a huge hit the next day, I was told later). We dulled my kitchen floor (already waxed for the holiday) with nut dust, cluttered every countertop with bowls and jars, and dirtied every cookie sheet we owned.

And when it was done, when we had finally finished the last nut, we laughed and drank eggnog from the back-porch crock and sang silly songs by candlelight (so none of us could see the mess we had made). And we—all five of us—went to bed mightily content.

Sometime during the night I woke, went downstairs to my destroyed kitchen, and sampled a piece of fudge cake. Standing in the square of windowed moonlight, I pondered philosophically just how it was that in the pursuit of the valid and religious I had somehow, over the years, failed to understand the value of the secular and human, had missed seeing that the one always serves the other.

I was peaceful in my new wisdom. The fudge cake in my mouth was still faintly warm and rich . . . until I bit down on the nuts. Then I laughed. Standing alone in my kitchen at two o'clock on Christmas Eve morning, I laughed. The pecans were stale! Mealy! Bitter to my tongue! But they were sweet as Christmas itself to my heart.

PRAYER FOR THIS WEEK . . .

Dear God, help me see beyond the surface of the things I do—especially those things I do with others. Sometimes I need reminding that memories are worth the mess. Help me recognize opportunities to interrupt my life to share special moments with the people I love.

KEEP ON KEEPING ON

Patsy Clairmont

....

With time and patience the mulberry leaf becomes a silk gown.

CHINESE PROVERB

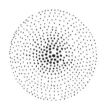

On a good day I am five feet tall . . . well, if I'm on a curb . . . I spiked my hair . . . and the wind is blowing in my favor. You would think with that kind of vertical brevity I couldn't block my own view, yet somehow I do.

Sort of like the Israelites in the book of Genesis in the Bible who, in search of the Promised Land, tripped over their own sandals, were easily distracted, and stayed spiritually dizzy in a cul-de-sac of excuses. They became known under Moses' leadership as people who wandered, whined, worried, and warred. And I've done all of those, which brings me back to my thoughts that, at my core, I am an Israelite. Not a Michigander (my birth state), not a Kentuckian (my parents' home state), not a Tennessean (my current home), but a burning-bush Israelite.

When Moses' people shook the dust of Egypt off their robes, they forgot to leave the spirit of slavery behind. I mean, I understand habits are hard to break . . . and I should know. When I first came to a fiery-bush understanding that God wasn't mad at me and that he was interested in my daily life, it still took me a long time to work through my addictions to caffeine, nicotine, television, and tranquilizers. They dominated my anxiety-ridden existence. Even after I found liberty from those out-of-control habits, I had only scratched the surface of changes I needed to make—ones that smacked familiar with the Exodus crowd.

WANDERING: I have never been a good goal planner. Some folks are. Me . . . not so much. But I have learned that without a purpose-driven mind-set, I'm left to squander my time. Haven't you come to the end of a day only to realize you lost precious hours to daydreaming, reruns, the Internet, etc.? I know I have. In fact, I lost years to mindless drivel, which is why I'm so determined today to "get stuff done" and be a life-long learner. No more wading knee-deep in the sand circling a mirage for me. Not me. I may stumble (repeatedly), but I'm headed toward the life-giving Promised Land.

WHINING: Yep, there, I said it. I'm whiny britches herself. I get why the Israelites complained that years of manna was a bit much. I mean, what are wafers without some Worcestershire to spice them up? When Les and I were in the poverty pay scale, we ate a lot of meat and sausages out of cans. You know the ones I mean. To this day I can't stand even the thought of either one. Yet if times became hard and provisions scarce, I'm sure I'd trade in my whine for a can of gratitude, then slice and dice those sausages into a tasty treat. Know what I mean?

WORRY: It's a habit like smoking in that it costs more than it's worth. It's a platform for anxiety. Wonder why your pantaloons are in a wad? Worry knots. It knots our nerves, our relationships, and our faith. It's just that simple and just that hard. To stop any habit takes time and effort, especially the sneaky intruder: worry.

So I'm ready: Are you? Let's roll up our sleeves and get busy because we have better things to do than fritter our time away with fruitless activity.

WARRING: God's people seem to have battle fatigue, but it's often from fighting each other. What's that about? Oh, how the enemy of our soul loves disputes. If there's a clamor, he's banging lids together to add to the intensity of the quarrels. It often starts with hurt feelings and assumptions that turn to resentment and bitterness. And Scripture warns us that bitterness will defile many. Not *might* but *will*. And note the word *many*. So don't be tempted to enter the fray; it's a trap. And we don't want to be a casualty.

Honestly, I think I might be overqualified for one of Moses' platoons. I wander, I whine, I worry, and I war (mostly inside myself). But I'm not giving up. I've made measurable progress, and I know I'm headed for the Promised Land. Together we will keep on keeping on.

PRAYER FOR THIS WEEK . . .

Lord, it's so easy for me to feel superior when I read about the Israelites and their missteps on their journey . . . until I realize I am just like them, often making the same kinds of mistakes. Show me the changes I need to implement so I can stop wandering, whining, worrying, and warring. Give me strength to persevere as I stumble along the road to the Promised Land.

Acknowledgments

Grateful acknowledgment is made to the following authors and publishers for permission to reprint copyrighted material:

Allen, Allison. "Going Small." Copyright © 2016. Used by permission. All rights reserved.

Bessey, Sarah. "Like a Child." Reprinted with the permission of Howard Books, a Division of Simon & Schuster, Inc. from *Out of Sorts* by Sarah Bessey. Copyright © 2015 Sarah Bessey.

Boyett, Micha. "An Invitation to Grow Up into Grace." From michaboyett.com. Copyright © 2014. Used by permission. All rights reserved.

Brett, Regina. "Get Rid of Things." From *God Never Blinks: 50 Lessons for Life's Little Detours* by Regina Brett. Copyright © 2010 by Regina Brett. Used by permission of Grand Central Publishing.

Carlson, Melody. "The Crazy Quilt." From *Patchwork of Love*. Copyright © 1997. Used by permission of the author. All rights reserved.

Clairmont, Patsy. "The Sleep That Nourishes Wisdom." From patsyclairmont .com. Copyright © 2013. "The Web" and "Keep On Keeping On" copyright © 2016. Used by permission. All rights reserved.

Craker, Lorilee. "All Things New." Copyright © 2016. Used by permission. All rights reserved.

Dale, Melanie. "Me, Too." Taken from *It's Not Fair* by Melanie Dale. Copyright © 2016 by Melanie Dale. Used by permission of Zondervan. www.zondervan.com.

Davis, Sarah Zacharias. "The Age of Friends." Excerpt from *The Friends We Keep: A Woman's Quest for the Soul of Friendship* by Sarah Zacharias Davis, copyright © 2009 by Sarah Zacharias Davis. Used by permission of WaterBrook Multnomah, an imprint of the Crown Publishing Group, a division of Penguin Random House LLC. All rights reserved. Any third party use of this material, outside of this publication, is prohibited. Interested parties must apply directly to Penguin Random House LLC for permission.

Dungy, Lauren. "Grace in Grief." Taken from *The Uncommon Marriage Adventure*. Copyright © 2014 by Tony and Lauren Dungy. Used by permission of Tyndale House Publishers, Inc. All rights reserved.

Fields, Leslie Leyland. "When Survival Isn't Enough: A Better Way to Live (and Die)." From www.leslieleylandfields.com. Copyright © 2015. Used by permission. All rights reserved.

Freeman, Emily P. "The Bench Dwellers." From *Simply Tuesday* by Emily P. Freeman. Published by Revell, a division of Baker Publishing Group. Copyright © 2015. Used by permission.

Gilliam, Connally. "Mastery?" From www.connallygilliam.com. Copyright © 2015. Used by permission. All rights reserved.

Griffin, Emilie. "The Discipline of Meditation." Text from pp. 27–31 [607 words] from *Wilderness Time* by Emilie Griffin. Copyright © 1997 by Emilie Griffin. Reprinted by permission of HarperCollins Publishers.

Haines, Amber C. "When You Want to Be the Fixer." From www.incourage.me. Copyright © 2015. Used by permission. All rights reserved.

Hatmaker, Jen. "A Family Crisis Manifesto." Adapted from jenhatmaker.com. Copyright © 2015. "Four Stages of Road Trip Management" and "God's Voice" copyright © 2016. Used by permission. All rights reserved.

Hudson, Sophie. "Twenty-Six Activities of Great Substance That I Enjoyed in High School." Taken from *Home Is Where My People Are*. Copyright © 2015 by Sophie Hudson. Used by permission of Tyndale House Publishers, Inc. All rights reserved.

Irving, Sharon. "Made New." From "Peace (Unplugged)" by Sharon Irving. Copyright © 2013. Used with permission. All rights reserved.

Kolbaba, Ginger. "Cinderella: Carpe Diem! (Carpe Pumpkin! Carpe That Shoe!)" From *Your Best Happily Ever After: Loving God's Beautiful Story for Your Life*. Copyright © 2015. Used by permission of Shiloh Run Press, a division of Barbour Publishing, Inc. All rights reserved.

Kopp, Heather. "How to Scream for Help." First appeared in *Huffington Post*. Copyright © 2013. Used with permission of author. All rights reserved.

Lau, Pamela Havey. "Developing Close Friendships." © 2015 Pamela Havey Lau. *A Friend in Me: How to Be a Safe Haven for Other Women* is published by David C. Cook. All rights reserved.

Lee, Jennifer Dukes. "The Extravagant Invitation We've All Been Waiting For." From jenniferdukeslee.com. Copyright © 2015. Used by permission. All rights reserved.

Mae, Sarah. "Paris Every Day." Taken from *Longing for Paris*. Copyright © 2015 by Sarah Mae. Used by permission of Tyndale House Publishers, Inc. All rights reserved.

Niequist, Shauna. "On Faith and Wind" from storylineblog.com. Copyright © 2013. "Use Your Words." From shaunaniequist.com. Copyright © 2015. "Throwing Candy" copyright © 2016. Used by permission. All rights reserved.

Nordeman, Nichole. "Valentines" and "Getting Lost, Staying Found" from *Love Story*. Copyright © 2012. Used by permission of Worthy Publishing, a division of Worthy Media, Inc. All rights reserved. "A Time To Tear; A Time to Mend" copyright © 2016. Used by permission. All rights reserved.

Norris, Kathleen. "Pride." From *The Cloister Walk* by Kathleen Norris, copyright © 1996 by Kathleen Norris. Used by permission of Riverhead, an imprint of Penguin Publishing Group, a division of Penguin Random House LLC.

Potts, Amy. "Hide Your Scars?" From artographicimages.com. Copyright © 2015. Used by permission. All rights reserved.

Raybon, Patricia. "Leading with Our Serve." From www.patriciaraybon.com. Copyright © 2015. Used with permission. All rights reserved.

Sandberg, Rebecca S. "Renewed Day by Day." Copyright © 2016. Used by permission. All rights reserved.

Sandberg, Sheryl. "What Would You Do If You Weren't Afraid?" Excerpt from *Lean In: Women, Work, and the Will to Lead* by Sheryl Sandberg with Nell Scovell, copyright © 2013 by Lean In Foundation. Used by permission of Alfred A. Knopf, an imprint of the Knopf Doubleday Publishing Group, a division of Penguin Random House LLC. All rights reserved. Any third party use of this material, outside of this publication, is prohibited. Interested parties must apply directly to Penguin Random House LLC for permission.

Topical Index

Endnotes

1. Chris Chase, "Serena Williams Was Viciously Booed, Trash-Talked at Hometown Tournament," *USA Today*, April 3, 2015, http://ftw.usatoday .com/2015/04/serena-williams-booed-miami-fans-simona-halep-miami -open.
2. Dan Ariely, *Predictably Irrational* (New York: HarperCollins, 2008), 21.
3. Susan Silk and Barry Goldman, "How Not to Say the Wrong Thing," *Los Angeles Times*, April 7, 2013.
4. C. S. Lewis, *A Grief Observed* (New York: HarperOne, 1996), 56–57.
5. E. Stanley Jones, *A Song of Ascents* (Nashville, TN: Abingdon, 1979), 190.

YOU'RE INVITED

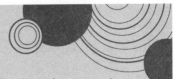

To be part of a community of real women who share their struggles and heartaches, hopes and dreams . . . a place where you can settle in and be accepted, just as you are. Join in through the resources below and at BELONGtour.com.

You Belong
An inspiring collection of reflections from a wide variety of women. Stories of identity, purpose, relationships, and living out your faith offer plenty of "me, too" moments. You'll laugh, wipe away an occasional tear, and gain fresh perspective.

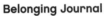

Belonging Journal
A space to capture your thoughts, prayers, and dreams. Encouraging verses and insightful quotes from a wide-ranging group of women are sprinkled across lined pages, designed to motivate and inspire you to pour out your heart . . . and explore what it means to belong.

Made to Belong
Go on a six-week journey to discover and pursue your unique calling. In this study of Habakkuk, you'll dig deep, try new things, and step out of your comfort zones as you step into an exciting and fulfilling future.

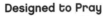

Designed to Pray
This eight-week adventure is filled with activities—everything from coloring pages to writing prompts to doodling. Here you'll find space to let go of your fears and expectations and discover what it means to engage with the One who loves you.

The BELONG Tour is an experience that challenges women to pursue their best life. It's a call for women of all walks of life and faith to connect more deeply. Get acquainted and find information on events and opportunities to be part of the BELONG community at BELONGtour.com.

CP1102

This is BIG.

Bigger than any one of us. *Because it's not about one of us; it's about all of us.*
When we gather, connect, and share, something happens. We change. We grow.
We want hearty exchanges with the people we love and safe places to fall.
We want to unpeel the layers and offer the best of ourselves.
Our best is rarely perfect, but that's OK.
We'll take real over perfect any day. And real happens here.

We have learned what it means to experience God's love in a real way
and renewed our belief in each other (and ourselves).

When we look at you, we see untapped power that can change the world.
Let's fan that flame and make things happen. We can do this. You are not alone.
We've readied a place for you to come in, to share, to heal, and to dance . . .

To BELONG.

JEN
hatmaker

ANGELA
davis

NICHOLE
nordeman

SHAUNA
niequist

SHARON
irving

PATSY
clairmont

At live events that bring women together in arenas across the country, remarkable
communicators gather with thousands of women to talk about how to live a fun,
faith-filled, purposeful life. There are plenty of personal stories, music, laughter, and
maybe even some tears in this Friday-night-to-Saturday event, where every woman
can find a place to belong.

**Get acquainted and find how you can be a part
of the BELONG community at BELONGtour.com.**

CP1103